"One of my favorite things about Christina Fox is her consistency. Everything she writes is clear on the gospel and passionately explains the truth that Jesus is both Lord and Christ and what that means for our lives. Her writing is a gift to the church! As we seek to follow Jesus we need reliable guides like Christina who believe the Bible and have the skill to apply its truth."

Gloria Furman
Author of *Alive in Him* and *Missional Motherhood*

"Many of us would say that we desire to have deep relationships with other women in our churches, but we would probably also have to admit that the reality of our experience often falls short of our aspiration. Sunday after Sunday, our interactions with one another rarely advance beyond the weather or the busyness of life. To help us out of this cycle of polite coffee-time chatter, *Closer Than a Sister* is both introduction and encouragement to authentic life in biblical community--where the joys and sorrows of my sisters in Christ can (and must!) become my joys and sorrows, too. Writing from years of intentional relationship-building, Christina Fox's words are wise and challenging. Fox lays out the priority of community, describes its beautiful contours, and gives her readers practical help to overcome its ever-present obstacles. Whether you read this book by yourself or with a group, your perspective on relationships in the church is sure to be enriched."

Megan Hill
Author of *Praying Together*; Contributor to The Gospel Coalition, Today in the Word, and CT Women; Editorial Board Member, and Christianity Today magazine.

"Christina Fox's new book, *Closer Than a Sister*, is a welcome invitation to seek meaningful and life-giving relationships in the church. Fox helps us understand our need for community, the various ways we can support and encourage one another, and the challenges we face as we build fellowship with one another. Rather than attempting to survive on surface-level friendships, Closer Than a Sister shows us how to live in biblical community with one another."

Melissa Kruger
Author of *The Envy of Eve* and
Walking with God in the Season of Motherhood

"In her latest book, *Closer Than A Sister*, Christina Fox through the use of biblical teaching, personal example, and practical teaching takes her readers by the hand and guides them through what the biblical and normal Christian life is like in the local church and outside of it. Wherever you are at in your Christian life, we all have a great need for one another, because we have a great ongoing need of Christ. Through Christ, God's people are wholly His, and He is wholly ours. As you read Christina's book, you'll be encouraged and along the way learn to be a true Christian friend and participant in your local church."

Dave Jenkins
Executive Director, Servants of Grace Ministries; Executive Editor,
Theology for Life Magazine and Co-Host, Equipping You in Grace Podcast

"Ask any woman if she wants friends (or even wants just one close friend) and she will likely tell you she does. The desire for relationships is part of what it means to be human and an image bearer of God. But so often we struggle. We want to be a good friend, but lack opportunities to meet people. We are hurt by friends. We hurt others. We have unmet expectations. Life in a broken world means our friendships aren't always what we want them to be, or what God intended. Christina Fox has written a beautiful and helpful book outlining a biblical definition of friendship, bringing in the familial language of scripture ("sister-friend"), showing us the Bible's definition of friendship, and pointing us towards the one Friend who will never leave us or forsake us. If you want to become a better "sister-friend" or find yourself longing for a friend, this book will encourage your soul."

Courtney Reissig
Author *Glory in the Ordinary*

"Closer than a Sister skillfully blends the glorious life-giving colors with the lackluster life-taking contrasts into a vivid portrait of gospel friendship. Every stroke is saturated with scripture with its aim towards gospel-centered application. And the real beauty of this book is the Jesus Christ is the centerpiece of what it truly means to live out the content of the covenant in the context of covenantal community."

Karen Hodge
PCA Coordinator of Women's Ministry;
Author of *Transformed: Life-taker to Life-giver*

"True side by side friendship is both a gift and a calling for Christians, yet it remains elusive and intimidating for many women. Here's a book that will encourage you in the beauty of Christ-centered relationships, and challenge you to take faith-driven steps of love in friend-ing others. *Closer Than a Sister* comforted me with the depths of Jesus' friendship for me, and compelled me outward with a renewed desire to be a godly friend to others."

Ellen Mary Dykas

Women's Ministry Director, Harvest USA; Author of *Sexual Sanity for Women: Healing from Sexual and Relational Brokenness* and *Sex and the Single Girl: Smart Ways to Care for Your Heart*

"In a day when discussions concerning women in the church and women's ministries, in particular, are at their zenith, Christian Fox has done us an enormous service by wedding a sound biblical theology of union with Christ to a sound biblical theology of fellowship--particularly as it relates to women in the church. In *Closer than a Sister*, Christina has done the hard work of laying the landscape while bringing the reader through all of the attendant obstacles that lead out to the green pastures of friendship building, maintaining, equipping and serving. This book is a timely, sound and engaging work from which any in the church may profit."

Rev. Nick Batzig

Pastor, New Covenant Presbyterian Church (PCA), Richmond Hill, Georgia and Editor, Reformation 21

"In *Closer than a Sister*, Christina Fox has painted a picture of biblical, God-honoring relationships among women in the church. She has then used that picture as a template to suggest how women can, because they are in union with Christ, live out this picture practically and by faith. Her honesty, transparency, and centeredness in God's Word make this a helpful read."

Chris Larson

President and CEO of Ligonier Ministries, Orlando, Florida

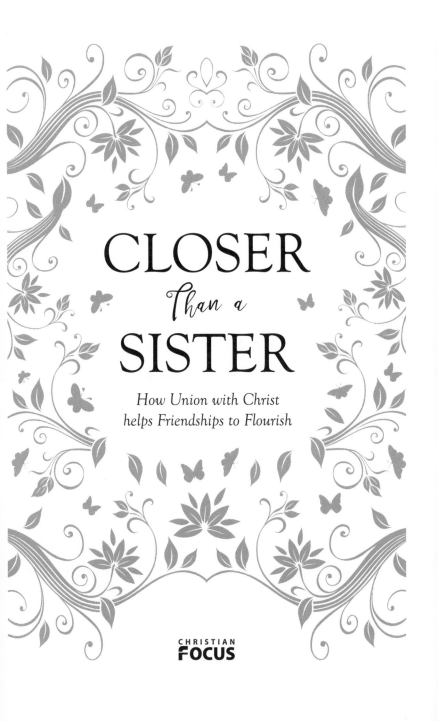

CLOSER
Than a
SISTER

How Union with Christ
helps Friendships to Flourish

CHRISTIAN
FOCUS

Copyright © Christina Fox 2017

paperback ISBN 978-1-5271-0032-9
epub ISBN 978-1-5271-0050-3
mobi ISBN 978-1-5271-0051-0

First published in 2017
by
Christian Focus Publications Ltd,
Geanies House, Fearn, Ross-shire
IV20 1TW, Scotland

www.christianfocus.com

A CIP catalogue record for this book is available
from the British Library.

Cover design by Pete Barnsley

Printed and bound by Bell and Bain, Glasgow

Contents

With much love to the community in my home: George, Ethan, and Ian.

Acknowledgements

THIS book is about community and books are community projects. I want to thank Christian Focus and Kate MacKenzie for taking on this project. They are a joy to work with and an encouragement to me as a writer. Thanks also to my editor, Anne Norrie, for her work on this project.

I had a team of friends who read and helped me edit the book and I am most grateful to each of them. Lisa Tarplee is a dear friend who knows my heart and read the book with diligence and an eye to detail. Maryanne Helms read and gave me helpful insight and input. I enjoyed our coffees together at Copper Coin (thank you, Copper Coin, for your excellent Cubano Lattes!). Thanks also to Rachel Miller, whose theological insight and wisdom steered me in the right direction. Nick Batzig was also a valuable resource and helped answer my theological questions. And my pastor, Tim Locke, thanks for your diligence in reading my book, encouraging me, and giving me your wisdom and insight.

I am thankful to Megan Hill for our monthly prayer phone calls. It is such a blessing to have a fellow writer who understands the writing process and all its challenges. I am thankful for her encouragement, prayers, and listening ear.

I am also grateful to my community past and present. I am thankful for all the lessons I learned about community during my years at Covenant College (go Scots!). I am blessed beyond measure by the community, mentoring, and discipleship I received during my years at Treasure Coast PCA. A special thanks to Marilyn Southwick, Linda Watts, Michele Eden, Misha Harris, and Martha Hansen for your friendship, support, and care. And to my new community at East Cobb PCA, thank you for taking me in and welcoming me with open arms.

I am thankful for all of my editors at the various websites and ministries I write for: Nick Batzig at Christward Collective, Lindsay Swartz at ERLC, Marshall Segal at Desiring God Ministries, Joe Holland at Ligonier, Leslie Bennett and Paula Marsteller at Revive Our Hearts, Kelly Givens at iBelieve, Melissa Kruger at TGC, Dave Jenkins with Servants of Grace, and Ruth Schwenk at For the Family. Your editing pushes me to be a better writer.

Thank you to Karen Hodge for her ongoing mentorship and encouragement. I am thankful for the opportunity to edit the PCA's women's ministry blog. Thank you, Karen, for all the opportunities, guidance, and support you've given me in ministry.

To the community in my home – George, Ethan, and Ian – thank you for allowing me time to write and for your constant prayers and encouragement. Love you!

Above all, I am thankful to God for adopting me as His child through Christ. I am thankful to Him for placing me in community, loving me through community, discipling me through community, and changing me through community. I look forward to the day when I can worship before the throne alongside my fellow brothers and sisters for all eternity.

Foreword

Jen Wilkin

I grew up in hymn-singing churches. As I read *Closer Than A Sister*, my mind kept summoning one remembered lyric in particular:

> *Blest be the tie that binds*
> *our hearts in Christian love;*
> *the fellowship of kindred minds*
> *is like to that above.*

It is a song about friendship among believers, and it rightly recognizes them for what they are: blessed bonds. Christian friendship is a gift, and one I have often counted too lightly.

I remember the first time I met Danna. Jeff and I walked into the Newlywed Class at Sugar Creek Baptist Church, freshly married and new to the area. All of five foot two, with long, dark curly hair, Danna introduced herself and chatted about anything and everything. She was from Colorado. She had graduated from Baylor University with a degree in Home Economics. She taught kindergarteners. She had been a cheerleader in high school. She liked to sew and to cook.

We had nothing in common.

I told Jeff on the car ride home, 'She's nice. We will not be friends.' It was not the last time I would be completely wrong.

We joined the church, and my path crossed with Danna's every Sunday. She had her first baby, and I watched her adjust to life as a mother. I remember sitting at my downtown office in a suit and heels, a few weeks pregnant myself, taking her call from the suburbs, filled with vivid descriptions of sleepless nights, showerless days, baby spit-up, and exploding diapers. I hung up the phone and thought, 'What on earth have I gotten myself into?' When my first child arrived a few months later, Danna smoothed the way with calm advice, regular visits, and food. I soon learned she was not just a talker, but a listener – and a good one. Our friendship began to grow.

It was Danna who talked me into volunteering at Vacation Bible School. 'I don't like kids,' I said. 'You'll be fine,' she assured me. With craft paper and glue, she transformed a Sunday school room into a jungle, complete with palm trees and a straw hut. As I cowered in a corner, kindergarteners swarming chaotically around me, she stepped into the room and uttered with the calm of a snake charmer, 'One, Two, Three – eyes on me.' Instantly, order ensued. I was dumbfounded. My friend was a wonder.

She knew things about getting stains out of laundry. She knew how to grow plants and how to quilt. She was always up for an adventure, always coaxing me out of my comfortable, introverted isolation. Come to the women's retreat. Come to Bible study. Let's take the kids to the splash park. Somehow my objections were always over-ruled. Thank God. Because God knew I needed a friend like Danna, whether I knew it or not.

When the storms of life came (and come they did) we navigated them together. The sharpest hurts, the hardest losses, the deepest disappointments. And also the wounds we gave each other – both those foolishly given in a moment of selfishness and those faithfully given as someone who wants what is best for her friend. I suspect that I have needed the lion's share of the faithful wounds of this friendship, the truth-telling that cuts deeply but is necessary for health. And I have needed steadfastness and grace. After the pattern of our Savior, she has given them.

Twenty-four years later, I recognize what I could not see that first day I met her. Danna and I shared the most important thing in common of all: We were sisters in Christ. It was a lesson I would learn again and again, as the Lord surrounded me with sisters – Lori, Kindra, Emily, Sally, Lindsey, Angie, Molly, Kristen, Anne, Caroline, Ann. Sisters to pray with, to mourn with, to laugh with, to share mutual comfort, to mine scripture with, to celebrate with and encourage, to join together in worship.

No other kind of friendship can offer the strength of Christian friendship. It is, just as the Bible promises, a 'cord of three strands, not easily broken' (Eccles. 4:12), joining those who enter it with the strength of a covenant-keeping God.

Christina Fox knows that this bond is both sacred and sacrificial. In *Closer Than A Sister* she offers insight into how we can weave the cords of our friendships to last through any season. Like all good gifts, Christian friendship is to be sought and stewarded with wisdom and grace. The benchmark of lesser friendships will not do. You hold in your hands a primer on how to weave (and allow yourself to be woven into) that blessed tie that binds.

JEN WILKIN
Author of *Women of the Word* and
None Like Him

MY HOPE
FOR YOU,
DEAR READER,
IS THAT YOU
WILL DESIRE
TO KNOW AND
BE KNOWN BY
YOUR CHURCH
COMMUNITY.

Introduction

'Two are better than one.'
Ecclesiastes 4:9

HOW many friends do you have? As you scroll through faces and names in your mind, it might be hard to narrow down and identify those friends. That's because the nature of friendship has changed so much in recent years. With the advent of social media, we have more 'friends' than we could ever have imagined just two decades ago. And that's just with Facebook. Add to that 'followers' from Twitter, Instagram, and Pinterest, connections with LinkedIn, and friends or Snapchatters on Snapchat, as well as all those connections through online games and other apps and your list could be quite long.

But are all of those people really your friends?

Which of them would come and bring you a meal if you were sick? Which of them would drop whatever they are doing and lend a helping hand? Which of them knows the real you, the you underneath the well-liked vacation photos, funny updates about the kids, and the happy face emojis? Which of them knows your heart struggles, your brokenness, and past pain? Which of them would encourage you with real gospel-centered hope when you needed it most?

It is those friendships I want to explore in this book. Real life, flesh and blood friendships. *Closer Than A Sister* is about friendship, but not just any friendship. The kind of friendship I explore in this book goes beyond that of borrowing sugar from the next door neighbor or going to lunch with a co-worker. It's a different kind of friendship than the one you make with a neighbor at the kid's bus stop or with the mom of your child's classmate at school. It's more than connecting with someone over similar interests and hobbies – though it may start there. This kind of friendship is one that only Christians experience and comes from our union with Christ through the gospel. *Closer Than a Sister* explores the relationships we have with others in the Body of Christ.

As I go through this book, I will often use the words 'community' 'sisterhood' and 'friendship' interchangeably. And though Christian community encompasses believers from all over the world (as well as those who are already in the presence of the Lord), when I talk about Christian community, I am referring to the local Body of Christ – the people in your church where you are a member. There are many friendships we have with believers who do not live near us and many of the characteristics we explore in this book will certainly apply and can be applied to those friendships but primarily, I will emphasize the friendships we have in real life with those in our local family of faith. Additionally, though our Christian community is made up of men as well as women, this book's emphasis is on relationships among women in the Body of Christ.

This book is divided into three parts. The first section focuses on the theological foundation for our Christian friendships, the origins of community, and how our unity in Christ creates unity with other believers. The main section of the book discusses what Christian friendship or sisterhood looks like by exploring various instructions in the New Testament written to the early church. The characteristics of friendship I explore are not an exhaustive list and certainly many others can be added. But for the sake of brevity, I highlight specific ones. Because we are sinful and fallen, the final section takes an honest look at the challenges we face in our relationships with sisters in the Lord and how the gospel speaks to those challenges.

My hope for you, dear reader, is that after reading this book you will desire to know and be known by your church community. I hope that you will see that you need Christian friendships and they need you as well. I hope that you will seek to deepen your friendships in your church and that such relationships would shine a light, reflecting Christ to the world.

Your sister in Christ,
CHRISTINA FOX

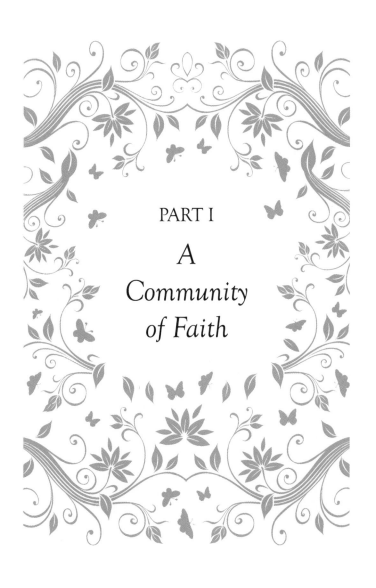

PART I

A
Community
of Faith

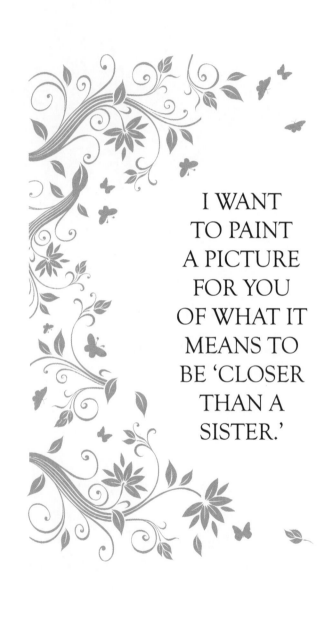

I WANT
TO PAINT
A PICTURE
FOR YOU
OF WHAT IT
MEANS TO
BE 'CLOSER
THAN A
SISTER.'

1

Made for Community

'No man is an island.'
JOHN DONNE[1]

BOTH of my children love to draw. For about five years they took a drawing class in the home of a local art teacher. There they learned the techniques of drawing. Whenever they started a new drawing, I couldn't always tell what it was supposed to be. That's because they began their drawing with basic shapes: triangles, rectangles, circles, and squares. Over time, as they continued their drawing, the shapes would transform into something familiar: an airplane, a lighthouse, an animal.

Learning about Christian friendship, learning to love and serve our sisters in covenant community, is a process,

---

1. http://www.famousliteraryworks.com/donne_for_whom_the_bell_tolls.htm

one which I will unpack as we move through this book. I want to paint a picture for you of what it means to be 'closer than a sister.' To do that, you'll have to follow me, stroke by stroke.

I want to paint the background first. To start, we have to go back to the beginning to understand the origins of relationships, the origins of community. Rather, we have to go back to *before the beginning*.

The Triune Community

'In the beginning was the Word, and the Word was with God, and the Word was God,' so begins the book of John. Such a proclamation tells us that Christ always is and always was. In fact John goes on to tell us that Christ was there when the world began, 'He was there in the beginning with God. All things were made through him, and without him was not any thing made that was made' (John 1:2-3). The Spirit was there as well, 'The earth was without form and void, and darkness was over the face of the deep. And the Spirit of God was hovering over the face of the waters' (Gen. 1:2).

Prior to the book of Genesis, before Adam and Eve, before creation and the fall of mankind, the three-in-one God existed. There has never been a time when God did not exist; He is the preexistent all eternal One. 'Before the mountains were brought forth, or ever you had formed the earth and the world, from everlasting to everlasting you are God' (Ps. 90:2). And God – Father, Son, and Holy Spirit – lived together for all eternity past as a community in perfect love, harmony, and unity.

This relationship among the triune Godhead is one of mutual glorification where the Father glorifies the Son,

'Father, glorify me in your own presence with the glory that I had with you before the world existed' (John 17:5), the Son glorifies the Father 'I glorified you on earth' (John 17:4), and the Spirit glorifies the Son 'When the Spirit of truth comes…He will glorify me' (John 16:13,14). Their relationship is one of self-giving love, each one delighting in, adoring, honoring, and treasuring one another. As Tim Keller wrote in *Reason for God*, 'Ultimate reality is a community of persons who know and love one another. That is what the universe, God, history, and life is all about.'[2]

Jonathan Edwards paints a beautiful picture of what it is like in heaven with the Trinity, 'There dwells God the Father, God the Son, and God the Spirit, united as one, in infinitely dear, and incomprehensible, and mutual eternal love. There dwells God the Father, who is the father of mercies, and so the father of love, who so loved the world as to give his only-begotten Son to die for it. There dwells Christ, the Lamb of God, the prince of peace and of love, who so loved the world that he shed his blood, and poured out his soul unto death for men. There dwells the great Mediator, through whom all the divine love is expressed toward men, and by whom they are communicated, and through whom love is imparted to the hearts of all God's people…There, in heaven, this infinite fountain of love – this eternal Three in One – is set open without any obstacle to hinder access to it, as it flows forever. There this glorious God is manifested, and shines forth, in full glory, in beams of love.'[3]

---

2. Keller, Timothy. *The Reason for God: Belief in an Age of Skepticism* (New York: Riverhead Books, 2008), p. 226.

3. Edwards, Jonathan. *Charity and Its Fruits: Christian Love as Manifested in the Heart and Life* (Lawton, OK: Trumpet Press, 2014), pp. 191-192.

Let that amazing description settle into your heart for a bit.

Doesn't it just give you pause, as you consider the great love of the Triune God overflowing? As beams of love shine forth throughout the halls of heaven? What's even more remarkable is that God has deigned to share this 'infinite fountain of love' with us!

The First Community

The first person to be invited into loving relationship with God was Adam. In Genesis 1, after God had created the heavens, the plants and animals, the sea creatures and flying birds, 'God said, "Let us make man in our image, after our likeness. And let them have dominion over the fish of the sea and over the birds of the heavens and over the livestock and over all the earth and over every creeping thing that creeps on the earth"' (1:26). Notice the use of the words 'us' and 'our' there. The Trinitarian God worked together in the act of creation. So God created Adam from the dust of the earth and put him in the garden. He gave him work to do, tending and keeping the garden. God then set boundaries for Adam and instructed him not to eat of the Tree of the Knowledge of Good and Evil (Gen. 2:17).

Notice also that God said, 'Let us make man in *our image, after our likeness*' (emphasis mine). We are image bearers. Of all the things that God made, only humans bear God's image. This doesn't mean that we look like Him in the physical way that our children look like us. God is a spirit and doesn't have a body like we do. However, we do image Him in His communicable characteristics.

The animals live their lives based on instinct. They eat out of instinct. They build shelters out of instinct. They protect themselves from predators out of instinct. Human beings are different. We are thinking and feeling beings. We have rational thought and can logically think through problems to find solutions. As image bearers, we have dominion over the created world. In this way, we represent God, demonstrating authority over the plants and animals. Like God, we are also creative, expressing ourselves in all forms of art. Unlike the rest of creation, we were made to commune with and have a relationship with our Heavenly Father. Because God is a Triune God and a community in Himself, we also reflect God by being in community ourselves, by forming relationships with others and loving other people.

That's why there was one thing in the garden that was not good. Everything God had made, He declared good. But there was one thing that wasn't, 'It is not good that the man should be alone; I will make a helper fit for him' (2:18). It wasn't enough that Adam had fellowship with the members of the Godhead. As an image bearer, Adam needed another human to reflect and bear the image of the community of God with him. God created Eve out of the rib of Adam and thus formed the first human community. 'Then the man said, "This at last is bone of my bones and flesh of my flesh; she shall be called Woman, because she was taken out of Man." Therefore a man shall leave his father and his mother and hold fast to his wife and they shall become one flesh. And the man and his wife were both naked and were not ashamed' (Gen. 2:23-25).

Adam and Eve lived in harmony with God. They enjoyed community together with their Maker, the intimate loving relationship that the members of the Godhead always knew. They experienced perfect love and joy with each other, speaking only words of kindness and goodness to one another. Adam desired only the best for Eve and she desired the same for Adam. Their relationship with God was perfect and complete. They loved God with all their heart. They found their joy and wholeness in being His children.

It is hard to imagine life in that perfect place. With all the heartache and conflict we experience in this world, it's hard to understand what Adam and Eve had in the garden with God and with each other. In my own home, we can't make it through the day without at least one argument or disagreement. It seems as though there is always someone with hurt feelings. We fail to serve one another and more often than not, seek our own best above everyone else. I pray every day that God would develop in me patience and love toward my family because it is not how I usually respond to them. To think that relationships were not always this way, that we were created to live in harmony with one another, is difficult to fathom.

Broken Community

The perfect love our first parents had for each other and for God ended the day they disobeyed God and ate from the tree which God had forbidden them to eat. In a moment, community was broken. They knew they were guilty and covered themselves in an attempt to hide what they had done. Their fellowship with one another was broken as they began blaming each other for what happened. Instead of being selfless toward each other, selfishness reigned in their hearts. Their fellowship with God was also broken as

He sent them away from the garden to toil and suffer the remainder of their days.

And as a result, they lost their intimate loving relationship with God and with each other.

Yet God didn't send them out of the garden without any hope. In Genesis 3:15 He promised, 'I will put enmity between you and the woman, and between your offspring and her offspring; he shall bruise your head, and you shall bruise his heel.' This wasn't a wish; it was a promise that was fact. Because God stated it, it would come to pass. In fact, the plan was already put into place before the world began (Eph. 1:4-6). In this promise, God gives us a glimpse of Jesus, the redeemer who would crush Satan and restore what Adam and Eve had broken. It's a promise that points to the meta-promise of Scripture that God would be our God and we would be His people (Gen. 17:7).

Our first parents left the garden with the lingering hope that one day a child would rescue them. Adam and Eve then went on to expand their broken community of two through children, creating a family. This new community soon felt the effects of the fall as one brother killed the other in a fit of jealous rage (Gen. 4).

A New Community

Mankind continued to spread throughout the earth, establishing fallen communities of broken people. God intervened when necessary to limit the expanse of the fall. At the Tower of Babel, He caused great confusion when everyone started speaking in a different language. No longer able to communicate, they separated and spread farther on the earth. In the days of Noah, evil was so pervasive that God brought a flood to destroy the earth, sparing a remnant, Noah and his family.

In Genesis 12, God announced a new community, one that would be great and one through whom He would bless the whole world. 'Now the Lord said to Abram, "Go from your country and your kindred and your father's house to the land that I will show you. And I will make of you a great nation, and I will bless you and make your name great, so that you will be a blessing. I will bless those who bless you, and him who dishonors you I will curse, and in you all the families of the earth shall be blessed"' (vv. 1-3). Abram took his family out of the land of Ur and obeyed God, following Him where He led.

In Genesis 15, God revealed to Abraham just how serious His covenant promise was. 'After these things the word of the LORD came to Abram in a vision: "Fear not, Abram, I am your shield; your reward shall be very great." But Abram said, "O Lord GOD, what will you give me, for I continue childless, and the heir of my house is Eliezer of Damascus?"…And he brought him outside and said, "Look toward heaven, and number the stars, if you are able to number them." Then he said to him, "So shall your offspring be." And he believed the LORD, and he counted it to him as righteousness' (vv. 1-2, 5-6).

Then God did something that would seem foreign to our modern experiences. He set up a series of animals cut in half and walked between them. This was a common custom of the day, a way to show the sincerity of a covenant one person made with another. In essence God was saying through this action, 'May the same thing happen to Me if I don't keep My end of the covenant.' O. Palmer Robertson defines a covenant as 'a bond in blood sovereignly administered.'[4] But with the making of this covenant, only God walked through the cut pieces. 'When the sun had gone down and it was dark, behold, a smoking fire pot and a flaming torch passed between these pieces. On that day the LORD made a covenant with Abram' (vv. 17-18). God Himself would make His promise come to pass, ultimately through the life, death, and resurrection of His Son, Jesus Christ.

God's plan continued to unfold as Abraham went on to have Isaac. Isaac then had twins, Jacob and Esau. Jacob fathered twelve boys who eventually became the nation of Israel. This nation soon found itself residing in Egypt after a severe famine. They grew and grew until the Covenant family was so large that Pharaoh enslaved them.

A Covenant Community

God used one of those Israelites to lead His people out of slavery and back to the land He promised their forefather Abraham. 'God spoke to Moses and said to him, "I am the LORD. I appeared to Abraham, to Isaac, and to Jacob, as God Almighty, but by my name the LORD I did not make myself known to them. I also established my covenant with them to give them the land of Canaan, the land in which they lived as sojourners. Moreover, I have heard the groaning of the people of Israel whom the Egyptians hold as slaves, and I have remembered my covenant. Say therefore

---

4. Robertson, O. Palmer. *Covenants: God's Way with His People* (Philadelphia: Great Commission Publications, 1978), p. 11.

to the people of Israel, "I am the LORD, and I will bring you out from under the burdens of the Egyptians, and I will deliver you from slavery to them, and I will redeem you with an outstretched arm and with great acts of judgment. I will take you to be my people, and I will be your God, and you shall know that I am the LORD your God, who has brought you out from under the burdens of the Egyptians. I will bring you into the land that I swore to give to Abraham, to Isaac, and to Jacob. I will give it to you for a possession. I am the LORD."' (Exod. 6:2-8).

As they began their journey across the desert, God instructed them in His law, showing them how to live in community as His chosen people. 'Thus you shall say to the house of Jacob, and tell the people of Israel: "You yourselves have seen what I did to the Egyptians, and how I bore you on eagles' wings and brought you to myself. Now therefore, if you will indeed obey my voice and keep my covenant, you shall be my treasured possession among all peoples, for all the earth is mine; and you shall be to me a kingdom of priests and a holy nation."' (Exod. 19:3-6).

The members of the covenant community were to live separate and distinct lives, different from the kingdoms around them. They were to worship God alone and follow His laws. They were to establish annual feasts and festivals to remind themselves of who God is and what He had done for them. They were God's chosen people, rescued from slavery, and freed by God's grace, 'For you are a people holy to the Lord your God. The Lord your God has chosen you to be a people for his treasured possession, out of all the peoples who are on the face of the earth. It was not because you were more in number than any other people that the Lord set his love on you and chose you, for you were the fewest of all peoples, but it is because the Lord loves you and is keeping the oath that he swore to your fathers, that the Lord has brought you out with a mighty hand and redeemed you from the house of slavery, from the hand of Pharaoh king of Egypt' (Deut. 7:6-8).

The rest of the Old Testament recounts how the nation of Israel failed time and time again to worship God alone. They failed to love Him with their whole heart and their neighbor as themselves. In time, the nation split into two kingdoms and eventually both were taken away into captivity. God's covenant community continued to violate His law. They needed rescuing. They needed someone to intervene, to restore their broken community, and to bring them back into right community with God.

Our Story

This brief overview of Biblical history is one many of us know. We've heard the stories in Sunday school and may have even read them to our children at bedtime. But this history is not just any story. It's not just words on a page. It is *our* story. I spent my childhood hearing my grandparents tell me stories of when they were children and young adults. Hearing about the adventures of their past, how they met their spouses, and the mark they made on the world was important to me because they were my family and part of me. These stories helped shape who I am. This is especially true of their spiritual history. Multiple times I heard the testimonies of how they came to faith and I thanked God that they did. For they then taught my parents God's Word and my parents in turn taught me.

It's even more important that we review and hear again and again the history of the family of God. We need to remember how God created mankind, what happened in the fall, and what God has done to redeem us from sin. We need to remember our family story, how we were created to live in unity with one another, and how sin broke that unity. Above all, we need to tell each other the good news that God created a new community through the blood of His Son, Jesus Christ.

Through Christ, we are part of the family of God. As members of the household of God, we are joined together with other members of that same community. The Christian life is one of community; a body of believers gathered together to worship and serve our triune God. The English poet John Donne is quoted as saying, 'No man is an island, entire of itself; every man is a piece of the continent, a part of the main.' As Christians, we are not islands either. We are united to the members of our covenant community. We can't live life on our own; we are in it together. What binds us together is Christ, who we will talk more about next.

Questions to Consider:

What does it mean to you that you were created for community, to image and reflect the three-in-one God? How does this impact the way you interact with other Christians in your church Body?

What do you think of the image Jonathan Edwards paints of our triune God in heaven?

Read 1 Peter 2:9-10. What stands out to you from what we have learned in this chapter? What common characteristics do we share with one another?

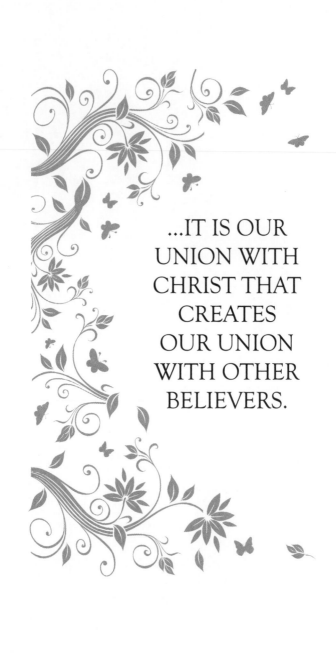

...IT IS OUR UNION WITH CHRIST THAT CREATES OUR UNION WITH OTHER BELIEVERS.

2

United to Christ and One Another

'Our community with one another consists solely in what Christ has done to both of us.'

<small>DIETRICH BONHOEFFER [1]</small>

AFTER living in the same house for fourteen years and in the same area for almost twenty years, my husband and I moved out of state last year. In the neighborhood we moved from, the houses were far apart and unless you happened to check your mail or walk your dog at the same time as a neighbor, you might never see them, much less

---

1. Bonhoeffer, Dietrich. *Life Together: The Classic Exploration of Faith in Community* (New York: Harper Collins, 1954), p. 25.

get to know them. We also lived in a community where there were more retirees than young families. So when we searched for a new house, we wanted to be somewhere where there were children, where the houses weren't far apart, and where people valued community.

All neighborhoods have their own unique community. Some have regular street parties. Others have book clubs, tennis teams, or weekly play groups for families with young children. Over the years, neighborhoods develop their own traditions and ways of doing things. Some become known as the 'neighborhood with the best Christmas light display.' When people live in a neighborhood for many years, there's a sense of unity with other families in the community. They are united by a common location and shared experiences.

In the Christian faith, believers are united together, not by location, common stage of life, or years of shared experiences, but by a shared Savior. This community is not made of bricks and mortar. It's not designed by an architect and constructed by a builder. It doesn't consist of tree lined streets, playgrounds, walking paths, or cul-de-sacs. This community is made up of people, created and built by God Himself through the blood of His own Son.

The Promised Redeemer

For generations, the Israelites failed to love God with all their heart. They turned away from Him to worship other gods. They didn't live as His chosen community. Despite this, God kept the promise He made in Genesis 3:15 and stepped into the world in human flesh. Jesus Christ, the Son of God, was born into this fallen and broken world so that He could redeem and restore us from our sin. Fully God and fully man, He came to redeem a people for Himself, people He had chosen before the world began.

Christ lived the perfect life we could not live, obeying the law in all things. 'For God has done what the law, weakened by the flesh, could not do. By sending his own Son in the likeness of sinful flesh and for sin, he condemned sin in the flesh, in order that the righteous requirement of the law might be fulfilled in us, who walk not according to the flesh but according to the Spirit' (Rom. 8:3-4). He endured temptation from Satan and never sinned. He was rejected, persecuted, suffered, and died to free us from our slavery to sin. When God the Father turned His back on Christ at the cross, Christ bore the weight of the wrath we were due. He experienced the separation from God that awaits all those who are not covered by faith. Because He was sinless, the grave could not hold Him and He rose from the dead and now sits at God's right hand, interceding for His people.

It is through faith in Christ – who has satisfied the justice of God on behalf of His people – all who believe are counted as righteous. When we believe, we are created anew, given new hearts that love God, and we become part of the community of faith.

Union with Christ

Through salvation, through Christ's atoning work for us on the cross, through the Spirit's work in our hearts making us alive to faith in that work, we are united to Christ. In fact, our union with Christ began in eternity past when God chose us in Christ, 'he chose us in him before the foundation of the world, that we should be holy and blameless before him' (Eph. 1:4). In union with Him we receive all the benefits of what He has done for us (i.e., justification, sanctification, and glorification). In our union with Him we are justified as God looks at us and sees not our filthy rags of sin, but Christ's robes of righteousness. In our union with Him we are sanctified as His Spirit works in our hearts, refining and transforming us into His likeness. We will be glorified through our union with Him when we are instantly made like Him on the last day.

Christ is united to the Father and the Spirit and we are united to the Father through faith in Christ by the Spirit at work in our heart. This union is mysterious and spiritual but it is a real union nonetheless. In this union, we are crucified with Christ, 'I have been crucified with Christ. It is no longer I who live, but Christ who lives in me. And the life I now live in the flesh I live by faith in the Son of God, who loved me and gave himself for me' (Gal. 2:20). We are made alive with Christ and raised with Him in newness of life: 'But God, being rich in mercy, because of the great love with which he loved us, even when we were dead in our trespasses, made us alive together with Christ – by grace you have been saved – and raised us up with him and seated us with him in the heavenly places in Christ Jesus' (Eph. 2:4-6). And we also share in His sufferings, 'But rejoice insofar as you share Christ's sufferings, that you may also rejoice and be glad when his glory is revealed' (1 Pet. 4:13).

In your study of the New Testament, you may have noticed phrases like 'in Christ' and 'in Him.' Whenever something is written multiple times like that, we should pay attention. These phrases, though short, refer to important truth. Paul used these phrases dozens of times in his letters to reference our union with Christ. 'But now in Christ Jesus you who once were far off have been brought near by the blood of Christ' (Eph. 2:13). 'There is therefore now no condemnation for those who are in Christ Jesus' (Rom. 8:1). 'Therefore, if anyone is in Christ, he is a new creation' (2 Cor. 5:17). 'The reason that the New Testament speaks again and again about being in Christ is that union with Christ is the fundamental reality of the Christian life.'[2]

In John 15, Jesus describes our union or connection to Him like that of a vine. 'I am the true vine, and my Father is the vinedresser. Every branch in me that does not bear fruit he takes away, and every branch that does bear fruit he prunes, that it may bear more fruit. Already you are clean because of the word that I have spoken to you. Abide in me, and I in you. As the branch cannot bear fruit by itself, unless it abides in the vine, neither can you, unless you abide in me. I am the vine; you are the branches. Whoever abides in me and I in him, he it is that bears much fruit, for apart from me you can do nothing' (vv. 1-6).

Only in union with Christ can we bear fruit. Only in union with Christ can we be His disciples. Only in union with Christ can we obey Him. Only in union with Christ can we do anything. Just as a branch receives its life and sustenance from the vine, we too receive our spiritual life

---

2. Ryken, Philip Graham (Editor). *The Communion of Saints: Living in Fellowship with the People of God* (Phillipsburg, NJ: P&R Publishing, 2001), p. 17.

and health from our union in Christ. We grow and bear fruit from the nutrients He provides. Our union with our Savior is our very life and breath.

So then, if we are not united to Christ, we are not saved, we have no forgiveness, and no redemption. If we are not united to Him, we will not be sanctified or transformed into His likeness. If we are not united to Christ, resurrection from death is not ours. Apart from union with Christ, we are lost and without hope.[3] Christ is everything; therefore, union with Him gives us everything.

Union with Others

When I got married, I was instantly part of a new family. My name even changed. I had a new sister-in-law and new mother-in-law and I became to them a sister and a daughter. I also became part of their family ways and traditions. I learned all the family stories, the family recipes, and how they liked to spend Christmas Day. And the same was true of my husband; he also received new family members upon our marriage.

Likewise, and even more so, it is our union with Christ that creates our union with other believers. 'Fellowship with other believers comes from having fellowship with God through Jesus Christ.'[4] The *Westminster Confession* puts it like this: 'All saints that are united to Jesus Christ their head by his Spirit, and by faith, have fellowship with him in his grace, sufferings, death, resurrection, and glory. And being united to one another in love, they

---

3. Ryken, p. 18.

4. Ryken, p. 16.

have communion in each other's gifts and graces; and are obliged to the performance of such duties, publick and private, as do conduce to their mutual good, both in the inward and outer man. Saints, by profession, are bound to maintain an holy fellowship and communion in the worship of God, and in performing such other spiritual services as tend to their mutual edification; as also in relieving each other in outward things, according to their several abilities and necessities. Which communion, as God offereth opportunity, is to be extended unto all those who in every place call upon the name of the Lord' (Chapter 26).

Our union with Christ creates our union with fellow believers. 'Only in Jesus Christ are we one, only through him are we bound together.'[5] Though we come to Christ as an individual, upon salvation we are immediately united to the members of the family of God. We are united by the blood of Christ to believers past, present, and future – to those saints in heaven and those yet to be born. We are united to those sisters and brothers in other parts of the world and those true believers who worship at the neighborhood church down the street. And one day, we will all worship our Savior together in the new heavens and the new earth.

A Spritual Community

By virtue of Christ's death and resurrection, He created a new community, His Body, His Bride, the Church. 'So then you are no longer strangers and aliens, but you are

---

5. Bonhoeffer, p. 24.

fellow citizens with the saints and members of the house-hold of God, built on the foundation of the apostles and prophets, Christ Jesus himself being the cornerstone, in whom the whole structure, being joined together, grows into a holy temple in the Lord. In him you also are being built together into a dwelling place for God by the Spirit' (Eph. 2:19-22). In most ways, it is a continuation of the old community, established with Abraham and the fulfillment of His promise to be our God and we His people. But instead of a community of only the Jewish people, this new community includes Gentiles. Through our union with Christ, we are grafted into the family tree, 'And if you are Christ's, then you are Abraham's offspring, heirs according to promise' (Gal. 3:29). We are one of those countless stars in the sky, a grain of sand on the seashore that together make up the people of God.

This community is not one we are physically born into, as we are with regard to our biological family. It is one we are born into spiritually. It even supplants familial ties (Luke 14:26, Matt. 12:48-50). This is why in some churches, church members refer to each other as 'Brother ____' and 'Sister ____.' This new community of faith is a family and we are all children of God, making the friendships we have with other women in the church even closer than a sister. 'I will be a father to you, and you shall be sons and daughters to me, says the Lord Almighty' (2 Cor. 6:18).

This new community also differs from that of the old community because rather than being centered on the Tabernacle and burnt sacrifices, this new community centers on Christ who has tabernacled among us and whose ultimate sacrifice supersedes that of sheep and goats.

Paul uses the image of a physical body to describe what this community looks like. 'For just as the body is one and has many members, and all the members of the body, though many, are one body, so it is with Christ. For in one Spirit we were all baptized into one body – Jews or Greeks, slaves or free – and all were made to drink of one Spirit' (1 Cor. 12:12-13). Paul goes on to say that each part of the Body is necessary and important; not one is better than the other (vv. 15-26). He tells us that we are so united and knit together that when one part suffers; we all suffer (v. 26).

What a unique community we get to be a part of! Like different colored threads, we are woven together to create a beautiful tapestry. My strand crosses with a sister in my church and our strands connect to your strand across the miles. We are knit together and part of the same whole.

A Union of Love

In John 17, before His betrayal and arrest, Jesus prays for the disciples and then for those who would believe in Him after them. 'I do not ask for these only, but also for those who will believe in me through their word, that they may all be one, just as you, Father, are in me, and I in you, that they also may be in us, so that the world may believe that you have sent me. The glory that you have given me I have given to them, that they may be one even as we are one, I in them and you in me, that they may become perfectly one, so that the world may know that you sent me and loved them even as you loved me.' (vv. 20-23).

In this, His High Priestly prayer, Jesus describes His union with His Father and in turn His union with the disciples and all those who would come to faith in the future. He prays that the union of His people would show the world who God is and His love for His people. This love that the Godhead shares is given to those who believe, 'the love with which you have loved me may be in them, and I in them' (John 17:26). We then learn, through the Spirit at work in us, how to extend that love to one another and to the world around us.

As John wrote elsewhere: 'We love because he first loved us' (1 John 4:19). Christ showed us what love looks like in the life He lived and the death He died for us. 'But God shows his love for us in that while we were still sinners, Christ died for us' (Rom. 5:8). He showed us that love is servanthood, the laying down of our life for the sake of others. 'By this we know love, that he laid down his life for us, and we ought to lay down our lives for the brothers' (1 John 3:16). All Christian acts of love are glory markers, pointing and reflecting back to the One who loved us first.

John 17 is also telling us that this love is the mark of a Christian. It is how the world will know that we are followers of Christ. Francis Schaeffer called this love the final apologetic. 'We cannot expect the world to believe that the Father sent the Son, that Jesus' claims are true, and that Christianity is true, unless the world sees some reality of the oneness of true Christians.'[6]

Our union with one another in the Body of Christ has a high and important goal: love. It's the inevitable result of being in union with our Savior. His love pours into

6. Schaeffer, Francis. *The Mark of the Christian* (Downers Grove, IL: InterVarsity Press, 1970), p. 27.

us and we then extend that love to others. As believers, because we are united to the same Savior, we experience and receive the same love from Him. And because He loves us, we then love one another.

As we go through this book, I will add the details to our painting. We will look at what our union with one another looks like within the Body and how it works out practically in our relationships with our sisters in the Lord. Specifically, we'll look at some examples from the New Testament church and how this new Christian community related to one another.

Questions to consider:

What does our union with Christ have to do with our relationships with other believers?

Read John 15:1-6 again. What does it look like to abide in Christ? How do you think abiding in Christ might have an impact on our relationships?

What do you think about Schaeffer's assertion that the love Christians have for one another is the final apologetic? Do you see this apologetic in your Christian circles? In the world? How about in your own life? How does your love for other believers tell others about Jesus?

Read 1 John 4:7-21. What does John say about God's love and the love we have for others?

...WE WERE
CREATED FOR
COMMUNITY
AND DESIGNED
TO REFLECT THE
THREE-IN-ONE
COMMUNITY
OF OUR
TRIUNE GOD.

3
The Sisterhood of Faith

*'Biblical community is first of all the
sharing of a common life in Christ.'*
JERRY BRIDGES[1]

THE day before my son was born, a hurricane blew into
our seaside town. This hurricane was preceded by another
only a couple of weeks before. Having two hurricanes land
on the same spot in the space of a month was overwhelming
to our community. Blue tarps covered nearly every other
house. The hospital where my son was born was damaged,
so much so that people recovering from surgeries were
lined up along the walls of the maternity ward. Power was
out for weeks in most homes and businesses.

---

1. Bridges, Jerry. *True Community: The Biblical Practice of Koinonia* (Colorado Springs: NavPress, 2012), p. 11.

Once I returned home from the hospital with our newborn, my husband tried to get our house back to normal. One day, I heard the sound of chainsaws out in the yard. 'Who is that?' I asked my husband. 'It's the guys from the fire department,' he responded.

At the time, my husband was a firefighter/paramedic for a city about an hour south of us. Fellow firefighters drove from their homes, at least an hour away, to come and help us cut up all the fallen trees and debris in our yard.

My husband often referred to the fire department as a brotherhood. These guys were bound together through their work rescuing and saving the lives of citizens. These guys (and sometimes girls, too) live together for twenty-four hours or more at a time. They train together, eat together, learn together, and in worst cases, are prepared to die together. As a result, they would do anything for each other. If a fellow firefighter was injured and in financial need, everyone on the department would write a check to help support them. If someone needed help with repairs at their home, everyone would show up at their house to lend a hand. And when one of them had fallen, whether on duty or not, they all showed up in their dress uniform to pay their respects and show honor to their fallen brother.

The brotherhood found in the fire service reveals a common bond forged through time spent fighting fires and saving lives. It is a similar bond, the bond of Christian sisterhood, we are going to explore in this chapter.

Friendship

Just what is a friend? When I looked up the word in the dictionary, the answers were interesting. The first definition was 'a person attached to another by feelings of affection or personal regard.' But for each of the definitions that followed, the meanings became less and less personal and more disconnected. 'A person who gives assistance.' 'Not hostile.' 'Member of the same nation.' And last, 'a contact on social media'.[2] Indeed, in our modern world, the word 'friendship' is hard to define. It doesn't hold the weight of meaning that it once did because we use it to refer to almost anyone, even those we have never met in person.

Friendships can form for many reasons and in multiple circumstances. Some friendships are formed through shared experiences, some through a common culture, and others through facing a common enemy (such as in the military). They can also form over stages of life (e.g., motherhood), common hobbies and interests, the workplace, and even location (like a college roommate or the next door neighbor). Such relationships grow over time and we often begin classifying them by attaching adjectives to explain what kind of friend a person is: new, old, close, dear, best, work, fishing, Facebook, etc. The Bible even implies that there are degrees of friendship. 'A man of many companions may come to ruin, but there is a friend who sticks closer than a brother' (Prov. 18:24).

In the middle of last century, C. S. Lewis described friendship as 'born at the moment when one man says to another "What! You too? I thought that no one but myself…"'[3] We've all had that 'You too?' moment with

---

2. Dictionary.com www.dictionary.com/browse/friend?s=t. Accessed 8/22/16.

3. Lewis, C.S. *The Beloved Works of Lewis* (New York: Inspirational Press, 1960), p. 255.

another person as we discovered a common interest that was important to us. In finding this mutual interest, we instantly felt less alone. No matter what the shared interest is, just knowing that someone else out there shared it with us, made us feel connected.

It may come as a surprise to know that the Bible uses the word 'friend' sporadically. Jesus referred to Lazarus as His friend (John 11:11). And we know they were close, for Jesus wept at Lazarus's tomb. A notable irony, Jesus referred to Judas as 'friend' when the soldiers came to arrest Him, 'Jesus said to him, "Friend, do what you came to do." Then they came up and laid hands on Jesus and seized him' (Matt. 26:50). In the book of John, Jesus referred to the disciples as His friends and described how far His friendship with them would go – to the point of death. 'This is my commandment, that you love one another as I have loved you. Greater love has no one than this, that someone lay down his life for his friends. You are my friends if you do what I command you. No longer do I call you servants, for the servant does not know what his master is doing; but I have called you friends, for all that I have heard from my Father I have made known to you' (John 15:12-15).

More often than not though, rather than using the words 'friends' or 'friendship,' the New Testament writers often used familial words to refer to other believers in the Body. '...for that indeed is what you are doing to all the brothers throughout Macedonia. But we urge you, brothers, to do this more and more' (1 Thess. 4:10). 'We know that we have passed out of death into life, because we love the brothers. Whoever does not love abides in death' (1 John 3:14). 'Therefore, my brothers, whom I love and long for, my joy and crown, stand firm thus in the Lord, my beloved' (Phil. 4:1). 'Do not rebuke an older man but encourage him as you would a father, younger men as brothers, older women as mothers, younger women as sisters, in all purity' (1 Tim. 5:1-2).

Sisterhood

The New Testament believers used familial terms because of their status as adopted children. Through our justification, we are adopted into the family of God. 'But when the fullness of time had come, God sent forth his Son, born of woman, born under the law, to redeem those who were under the law, so that we might receive adoption as sons. And because you are sons, God has sent the Spirit of his Son into our hearts, crying, "Abba! Father!" So you are no longer a slave, but a son, and if a son, then an heir through God' (Gal. 4:4-7). Christ is our elder Brother, with whom we are heirs, together with all the saints. J. I. Packer asserted in his book, *Knowing God,* that adoption 'is the highest privilege that the gospel offers.'[4] He also wrote, 'Adoption is a family idea, conceived in terms of love, and viewing God as father. In adoption, God takes us into his family and fellowship – he establishes us as his children and heirs. Closeness, affection and generosity are at the heart of the relationship.'[5]

I still believe that the word 'friend' is appropriate to describe our relationships with others in the church.

---

4. Packer, J.I. *Knowing God* (Downers Grove, IL: InterVarsity Press, 1973), p. 206.

5. Packer, p. 207.

However, because the word has become so muddied in recent years, I think that sisterhood is almost a better description. Though friends we meet in college or at work or at our child's preschool will come and go, we know that our link to our biological relatives is something that cannot be severed. We are tied to them through blood. In a similar way, we are united to our sisters in Christ through the blood of our Savior and our union is forever.

So I will use the word 'sister' or 'sister-friend' to refer to the Christian friendships we have in the church. I want to do that to ensure that you know I am not talking about relationships that are centered only on enjoying the same activities. Christian friendship goes deeper than just sharing a common love of sports, fashion, music, or work. In fact, I'll unpack what I mean by that next.

Fellowship of Believers

More so than using the word 'friendship,' in the New Testament, the Greek word 'koinonia' is used to refer to the new relationship formed among believers united in Christ. It is most often written as 'fellowship' in our Bibles. When the church first began, after Christ had risen from the grave and ascended into heaven, and following the miraculous and Spirit-filled happenings on Pentecost, Luke tells us, 'And they devoted themselves to the apostles' teaching and the fellowship, to the breaking of bread and the prayers' (Acts 2:42).

Often when we think of fellowship in the church, we think of Wednesday night spaghetti dinner in the church fellowship hall. Or we might think of the time between Sunday school and worship where we stand around with our coffee and catch up on each other's week. The fellowship described in the New Testament goes deeper than chatting over a cup of coffee. It's more than talking about the latest remarkable thing our child did with other ladies before Tuesday morning Bible study begins. And it's far more than leaving a comment on someone's status update on social media, no matter how spiritual the comment may be.

The fellowship that the Bible describes in Acts is that of sharing a common life together. As Jerry Bridges notes in his book, *True Community*, 'The first Christians of Acts 2 were not devoting themselves to social activities but to a relationship – a relationship that consisted of sharing together the very life of God through the indwelling of the Holy Spirit. They understood that they had entered this relationship by faith in Jesus Christ, not by joining an organization. And they realized that their fellowship with God logically brought them into fellowship with one another. Through their union with Christ, they were formed into a spiritual organic community.'[6]

Sharing a common life together is not about doing activities but about sharing *life*. Spiritual life. It is about working together to bring about God's Kingdom purposes. It is about serving together, helping each other through trials, lifting each other up when we fall, praying for one another, urging one another on in the faith. And ultimately, it is reflecting Christ in our love for one another, imaging Him to the fallen world around us.

It all starts with our own friendship with God – our own fellowship with God. We give and receive from Him.

---

6. Bridges, Jerry. *True Community: The Biblical Practice of Koinonia* (Colorado Springs: NavPress, 2012), pp. 10, 11.

We give Him our burdens and He gives us His grace, rest, and strength. We receive from Him spiritual nourishment and then pour it out to other believers. They in turn also receive from God and pour it out into our lives. It is a constant flow, an unceasing giving and sharing of God's love and grace with one another.

Two-way Fellowship

J. I. Packer describes Christian fellowship like this, 'Christian fellowship...is a two-way traffic which involves both giving and taking on both sides. It is, first, a sharing with our fellow-believers the things that God has made known to us about himself, in hope that we may thus help them to know him better and so enrich their fellowship with him...Fellowship is, secondly, a seeking to share in what God has made known of himself to others, as a means to finding strength, refreshment, and instruction for one's own soul. In fellowship, one seeks to gain, as well as to give...Thus, Christian fellowship is an expression of both love and humility. It springs from a desire to bring benefit to others, coupled with a sense of personal weakness and need. It has a double motive – the wish to help, and to be helped; to edify, and to be edified....It is a corporate seeking by Christian people to know God better through sharing with each other what, individually, they have learned of him already.'[7]

Now this doesn't mean that fellowship *can't* occur at the weekly spaghetti dinner or over a cup of coffee.

---

7. Packer, J. I. *God's Words: Studies of Key Bible Themes* (Grand Rapids: Baker Book House, 1981), pp. 195-196.

Rather, we can't mistake superficial engagement with other believers as the same kind of fellowship found in Scripture. However, church meals and cups of coffee (or tea!) can be a means and can be used to cultivate fellowship. We can take those opportunities, like a church dinner, to pour into the lives of others. We can share our mutual struggles, joys, challenges, loves, trials, and hopes with one another. We can speak to one another of our shared hope in Christ, what He has done for us and in us. That's when real *koinonia* or fellowship takes place.

We Need Fellowship

I've talked to people who shrug at the idea of commitment to a local body of believers. They think of church as a place you go to hear an inspiring message. They go for a pick-me-up to inspire them for the coming week at work or for a boost of self-help instruction to encourage them at the end of a difficult week. And if they don't have time to attend church on Sunday morning, they can always listen to a podcast or read a blog post. This kind of half-hearted involvement with the church misses the purpose of the church altogether. They don't realize their vital need for the Body of Christ.

Because we were created for community and designed to reflect the three-in-one community of our Triune God, we need to be in spiritual community with our church family and share our common life together. We need flesh and blood, face to face, interactions. Online relationships and interactions are no substitute. We simply cannot know others or be known in a virtual world. We also cannot know or be known when we slip into the last row of church ten minutes after it starts and leave right after the benediction. We cannot give or receive true Christian fellowship if we are not actively engaged in sharing a common life with our family in the Lord.

God uses our fellowship with one another to encourage us spiritually. He also uses us in one another's sanctification as we point out the truth to each other. He uses us to carry one another's burdens as we help each other in practical ways. He uses our prayers for one another to carry out His will. He uses us to disciple and to teach one another in the Word and the way of faith. We need that community and without it, we are weakened.

The book of Hebrews was written to a people who were in the midst of persecution and suffering. They were losing their jobs and possessions because of their faith. Some were being martyred. The writer to the Hebrews wanted to encourage them with eternal hope to stand firm in their faith, to cling to God's promises, and to remember what awaited them on the other side.

Because they were being persecuted, the Hebrew believers were tempted to stop meeting for worship. Perhaps they thought that if they stopped associating themselves with other believers, the persecution would end. But the writer to the Hebrews encouraged them otherwise saying, 'And let us consider how to stir up one another to love and good works, not neglecting to meet together, as is the habit of some, but encouraging one another, and all the more as you see the Day drawing near' (10:24-25).

We can't neglect to meet together. We must remain united and connected to one another, mutually encouraging and stirring one another on in the faith. As Nancy Guthrie wrote concerning this passage in Hebrews, 'Christianity is corporate. There are no lone rangers in the body. We need each other. And we need to encourage each other. Maybe you are full of courage today. If so, then offer some of yours to someone else. Don't operate in the body looking only to get your needs met. Look for needs that you can uniquely meet, and in the process you'll find your needs uniquely met.'[8]

As we seek to love and serve our sisters and they in turn love and serve us, we are living out our union with Christ. We are reflecting the triune community. We are showing the world the love of Christ. 'By this all people will know that you are my disciples, if you have love for one another' (John 13:35).

Abide in Christ

Lastly, our fellowship with other sisters in our church must begin with and flow out of our fellowship with God. Our friendship with other sisters is rooted in our friendship with our Savior. We cannot love and serve one another apart from our union with Christ. 'Only to the extent that we understand and appropriate the life we have in Christ will we be able to share that life with others.'[9] Once we seek to do fellowship apart from our union in Christ, our fellowship ceases to be spiritual and becomes just like any other friendship.

Jesus calls us to abide in Him for apart from Him we can do nothing (John 15:5). This requires that we keep the truths of the gospel ever before our eyes. We must

8. Guthrie, Nancy. *Hoping for Something Better: Refusing to Settle for Life as Usual* (Colorado Springs: Salt River, 2007), p. 115.

9. Bridges, Jerry. *True Community: The Biblical Practice of Koinonia* (Colorado Springs: NavPress, 2012), p. 32.

remember who we are in Him, what He has done for us at the cross, and what He has promised us as His covenant children. We must remember that all we are and all we have comes to us by His grace. In keeping our gaze fixed on Christ, we will remember our union with Him.

How do we do that practically? There are no new answers to that, just what we already know. We read and study God's word. We commune with Him in prayer. We participate in worship and the sacraments. We rest in the knowledge that Christ is the author and finisher of our faith and that He will complete the work He began in us. Jerry Bridges notes, 'in order to *abide* in Him, we must *know* that we are in Him. Only as we realize in the deepest levels of our understanding that we are branches of the true Vine, Jesus Christ, will we be able to confidently look to Him for all the resources we need to practice fellowship as it is meant to be practiced.'[10]

As sinners, because we are easily distracted and prone to forgetfulness, there will be times when we forget who we are and whose we are. We will forget that we were created for community. We will forget that Christ has set us free from sin. We will forget our union with Him and our union with others in the Lord. The glorious truth of the gospel is that our union with Christ is not contingent upon our grasp of Christ but of His grasp of us. Though we stumble and shift our gaze from Him, He never lets go of us. Though we forget His promises, He never forgets His covenant with us. Once united to Him, always united to Him.

---

10. Bridges, Jerry. *True Community: The Biblical Practice of Koinonia* (Colorado Springs: NavPress, 2012), p. 32.

Yes, we often forget and stray but God always draws us back to where we belong. So dear sisters, when you find yourself struggling to engage in community with others, when you find yourself spiritually weak, when you feel disconnected and all alone, turn back to the Lord. Abide in Him. Fellowship with Him through His word. And then seek encouragement from the sisterhood of faith. 'But if we walk in the light, as he is in the light, we have fellowship with one another, and the blood of Jesus his Son cleanses us from all sin' (1 John 1:7).

In these first few chapters, I've painted the background of our canvas. We've looked at the theological foundation for community and Christian friendship. I added some depth and color to it by defining friendship. Now I want to paint the portrait of friendship by looking at specific aspects of friendship among women in the church. How do we live out our sisterhood in the Lord?

Questions to Consider:

How does the Biblical description of fellowship differ from what you think of? How does it differ from the relationships we might have with others in social media?

Have you ever craved something more than superficial talk with other believers? Have you ever wanted to be known and encouraged by others in the faith?

Read Romans 1:7-15. What is Paul's relationship with the Roman church? Do you see a desire to mutually give and receive? Do you see his longing to be with them in person, to engage in face to face fellowship?

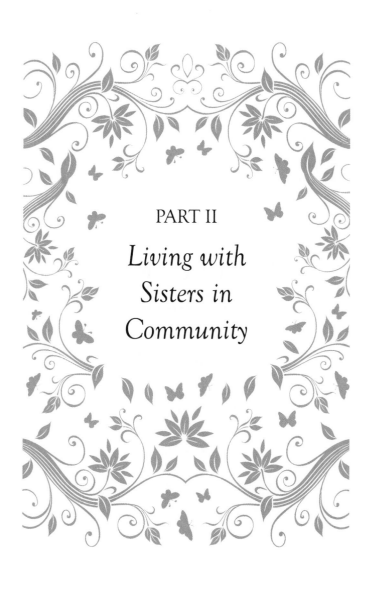

PART II

*Living with
Sisters in
Community*

WHEN WE
HELP OUR
SISTERS BY
MEETING THEIR
PHYSICAL
NEEDS, WE
ULTIMATELY
REFLECT WHAT
OUR SAVIOR
HAS DONE
FOR US.

4

Sisters Help Each Other

'...through love serve one another.'
GALATIANS 5:13

I first encountered Christian community or Christian friendship the year my father lost his job. It was a time of an economic recession. I was sixteen and battling emotional despair that at times paralyzed me. I felt alone and uncertain about our family's future. Would my sister and I be able to stay in Christian school? How would we afford food? Gas? The tension in our house was high as every conversation centered on my father's job hunt, bills, and what we could or could not afford.

One cold November evening I heard the doorbell ring. We were not expecting company. I looked through the tiny round hole in the front door and saw a face I recognized. It was a friend from youth group. As I opened the door,

I thought, 'Why in the world is she at my house? She lives far from here.' With the door open wide, I saw that there were more gathered there on the doorstep than that one friend. There were several friends standing there, all holding grocery bags.

They came into the house and stopped at the kitchen table. 'We know you are going through a rough time right now and we didn't want you to be without Thanksgiving dinner,' one of my friends announced. As we unpacked the bags, I found a turkey, stuffing, pie, and ingredients for side dishes – everything we would need to make a Thanksgiving meal. I was overwhelmed by their kindness and thoughtfulness. All this from a group of teenagers!

That day, I encountered true Christian community; true gospel friendship and it changed me. That act of kindness is something I never forgot. It helped open my eyes to see what Christian community is all about.

Helping Our Sisters

The first aspect to Christian community I want to explore is that of helping one another. It is a good place to begin as we consider ways we can grow in our sisterly love for one another in the church.

As children of the Father, we need to look out for one another. When a sister is in need, we help meet that need. That's what my friends in my youth group did for me and my family all those years ago.

The kind of help a person needs will vary from friend to friend but it includes providing for one's physical needs, helping and serving with our time and labor, and sharing with them what we have. It means providing a meal to a sister-friend who has just had a baby. It means lending a car when a friend can't afford to repair their broken down one. It means offering to babysit when a friend is sick. It means sharing clothing, toys, and other material possessions. It may even mean opening our home when a friend loses theirs. 'So then, as we have opportunity, let us do good to everyone, and especially to those who are of the household of faith' (Gal. 6:10).

Helping our sisters in Christ isn't simply a nice thing to do. It's not just a good deed done out of the kindness of our heart. It's a natural overflow of our connection to one another in Christ – originating in our union with Christ Himself.

That's what happened following Pentecost. Thousands came to faith in Christ and at once they were united to one another. Those first Christians began meeting together for worship, hearing the word preached, celebrating communion, and praying together. They enjoyed sweet fellowship with one another. They lived life together, so much so that they shared what they had with others in need, even to the point of selling their belongings to provide for others. 'They devoted themselves to the apostles' teaching and to fellowship, to the breaking of bread and to prayer. Everyone was filled with awe at the many wonders and signs performed by the apostles. All the believers were together and had everything in common. They sold property and possessions to give to anyone who had need. Every day they continued to meet together in the temple courts. They broke bread in their homes and ate together with glad and sincere hearts, praising God and enjoying the favor of all the people. And the Lord added to their number daily those who were being saved' (Acts 2:42-47).

Following the Dispersion, when Christians were persecuted in Jerusalem and fled the city, churches began to grow and spread. The apostles went on missionary journeys throughout the Mediterranean, sharing the good news of the gospel wherever God led them. These churches, though spread far apart by miles and even by culture and custom, would send money to other churches in need.

Philippi was one such church, and one that Paul planted. This church stands out in Paul's mind as one who was generous in meeting his own personal needs. In Philippians 4, Paul expressed his gratitude to the Philippian church for how they provided for him. He was imprisoned and, in those days, prisons did not provide food or anything else for their prisoners. It was expected that friends and family members would bring a prisoner whatever they needed. 'And you Philippians yourselves know that in the beginning of the gospel, when I left Macedonia, no church entered into partnership with me in giving and receiving, except you only. Even in Thessalonica you sent me help for my needs once and again. Not that I seek the gift, but I seek the fruit that increases to your credit. I have received full payment, and more. I am well supplied, having received from Epaphroditus the gifts you sent, a fragrant offering, a sacrifice acceptable and pleasing to God' (4:15-18).

When we share what we have, or provide for a sister's physical needs, the gift is a fragrant offering to God and pleasing to Him. The love and care we give to someone else is ultimately a gift given to God. The author to the Hebrews puts it this way, 'Do not neglect to do good and to share what you have, for such sacrifices are pleasing to God' (13:16). And this gift is multiplied. It is scattered like seed which bears fruit of thanksgiving to God in the heart of the receiver. As Paul told the church at Corinth about what would happen when they supplied funds for the needs of other churches, 'He who supplies seed to the sower and bread for food will supply and multiply your seed for sowing and increase the harvest of your righteousness. You will be enriched in every way to be generous in every way, which through us will produce thanksgiving to God. For the ministry of this service is not only supplying the needs of the saints but is also overflowing in many thanksgivings to God' (2 Cor. 9:10-12).

A Reflection of our Savior

God's word is replete with admonitions to help and serve others. Israelite law made provisions for meeting the needs of the widow and the poor (Lev. 19:9-10). The deaconate originally began to meet such needs in the early church (see Acts 6). Indeed, God's heart for those in need is voiced in the vivid words of Isaiah, 'Is not this the fast that I choose: to loose the bonds of wickedness, to undo the straps of the yoke, to let the oppressed go free, and to break every yoke? Is it not to share your bread with the hungry and bring the homeless poor into your house; when you see the naked, to cover him, and not to hide yourself from your own flesh?' (58:6-7).

Our Savior came to serve those in need. 'For even the Son of Man came not to be served but to serve, and to give his life as a ransom for many' (Mark 10:45). He met the physical needs of the hungry. He cast demons out of the possessed. He healed the sick and befriended the outcast. Ultimately, Jesus met our greatest need, forgiveness of sins, when He died on the cross as our substitute.

On the night of His betrayal, Jesus did something unthinkable. He got down on hands and knees and washed the disciples' feet. 'During supper, when the devil had already put it into the heart of Judas Iscariot, Simon's son, to betray him, Jesus, knowing that the Father had given all things into his hands, and that he had come from God and was going back to God, rose from supper. He laid aside his outer garments, and taking a towel, tied it around his waist. Then he poured water into a basin and began to wash the disciple's feet and to wipe them with the towel that was wrapped around him' (John 13:2-5).

This was a servant's job; a job for the non-Jew. It was a degrading job. That the God of the universe would lower Himself to serve in this way is remarkable and humbling. It was an act of love for His disciples, including His enemy, the one who was about to betray Him. When Jesus finished washing their feet He got up and said, 'Do you understand what I have done to you? You call me Teacher and Lord, and you are right, for so I am. If I then, your Lord and Teacher, have washed your feet, you also ought to wash one another's feet. For I have given you an example, that you also should do just as I have done to you. Truly, truly, I say to you, a servant is not greater than his master, nor is a messenger greater than the one who sent him' (John 13:12-15).

Our Lord set an example for us of what it means to serve one another. When we help and serve our sisters by meeting their physical needs, we ultimately reflect what our Savior has done for us. 'By this we know love, that he laid down his life for us, and we ought to lay down our lives for the brothers. But if anyone has the world's goods and sees his brother in need, yet closes his heart against him, how does God's love abide in him? Little children, let us not love in word or talk but in deed and in truth' (1 John 3:16-18).

Christ left the grand palaces of heaven, lowered Himself by taking on human skin and bones and lived in this sin-stained world. He gave up His very life for us and calls us to do the same. 'Have this mind among yourselves, which is yours in Christ Jesus, who, though he was in the form of God, did not count equality with God a thing to be grasped, but emptied himself, by taking the form of a servant, being born in the likeness of men. And being found in human form, he humbled himself by becoming obedient to the point of death, even death on a cross' (Phil. 2:5-8).

As we help and serve our sisters, we image our Maker and Creator. Tripp and Lane remind us, 'When you and I serve, we are living out what God has made us to be, servants. It is when we are serving that we are most like the Trinity. Father, Son, and Spirit redeemed a fallen world through service and sacrifice. There is nothing more God-like than serving others.'[1]

What Keeps Us From Helping?

Helping others is always a sacrifice. It is a sacrifice of time, money, energy, and goods. It's never easy and it's often messy. Because of this, we often hesitate to help or our help only goes so far. We might hear that someone in our

---

1. Lane, Timothy S. and Tripp, Paul David. *Relationships: A Mess Worth Making* (Greensboro, NC: New Growth Press, 2006), p. 127.

church community is struggling and we might say, 'I'm sorry to hear that you lost your job. I will be praying for you.' Or we might be willing to write a check but investing our time in someone else is just too much of a sacrifice.

Sister-friends, because we are united together as sisters in the Lord, when one of us hurts, we all hurt. Therefore we need to do more than pray. We also need to act. Such acting reveals the love of Christ in us, and it ultimately points the world to our unity in Christ.

For many of us, our time is a closely guarded commodity. We spend it on ourselves and our family and then we are all out. To interrupt our schedules in order to visit someone who is sick or to bring food to someone who needs it or to take a weekend to serve someone's physical needs, that goes beyond our comfort level. But when a sister is in need, God calls us to give whatever we have. We are to give as Christ has given, even if it means interrupting our plans. In fact, as Deitrich Bonhoeffer pointed out, God will often interrupt our plans, providing us opportunities to serve others:

> We must be ready to allow ourselves to be interrupted by God. God will be constantly crossing our paths and canceling our plans by sending us people with claims and petitions. We may pass them by, preoccupied with our more important tasks, as the priest passed by the man who had fallen among thieves…But it is part of the discipline of humility that we must not spare our hand where it can perform a service and that we do not assume that our schedule is our own to manage, but allow it to be arranged by God.[2]

---

2. Bonhoeffer, p. 99.

Sometimes we may think that we have nothing to offer. Perhaps we are struggling with our own physical needs, how could we possibly help another friend? The truth is, there is always something we can do or give. The first step is to be willing to help and serve; to have a heart that is open to give and share.

What Keeps Us From Asking?

It is also equally important that we reach out and ask for help from our sister-friends when we are in need. When we have lost a job or are sick and can't get out of bed to get the kids off to school or a pipe breaks and we have no money for repairs, we need to reach out to our church Body and ask for help.

This is a hard step for many of us. I, for one, don't like to ask for help. But often, I'm forced to. My husband travels for work and inevitably something will break while he is gone. Many times I've had to reach out to my community and ask for help. I don't like to because I feel like a burden and an inconvenience.

When my oldest son was a baby, I was sick and couldn't get out of bed. My husband could not take off from work to stay home. He suggested I call someone from church to come over and help me. I hesitated because I didn't want to trouble anyone. I felt embarrassed that I needed help. Then I got a call from an older friend who told me that my husband had contacted her and she was on her way to spend the day at my house. And I was so grateful that she did!

We live in a culture of independence; we are wired to do things on our own. We spend our teenage years counting down the days until we are old enough to move out and make our own decisions. To depend or rely on anyone else is foreign to us. But we have to remember that God did not create us to live in isolation. We weren't made to be autonomous. We were created to be dependent upon God and mutually dependent upon others in the Body of Christ. We were created to live in community and to need one another. When we are struggling and in need of help, we should reach out to a gospel friend and say, 'I really need help. Could you come spend time with my children?' Or 'I'm recovering from surgery and can't get out of bed. Could you come over and help me?'

Because we are united to our sisters through the blood of Christ, when a sister in Christ helps us, it is Christ helping us. Such community love and service is God loving us through others. 'The prisoner, the sick person, the Christian in exile sees in the companionship of a fellow Christian a physical sign of the gracious presence of the triune God. Visitor and visited in loneliness recognize in each other the Christ who is present in the body; they receive and meet each other as one meets the Lord, in reverence, humility, and joy. They receive each other's benedictions as the benediction of the Lord Jesus Christ.'[3]

This means we need to have a church culture where people are not ashamed to reveal that they are hungry or having difficulty paying bills or that their car has broken down and they can't afford the repairs. It should be the normal way of things that not only do we share our health concerns with others in our church, but also that we tell others about our physical needs. Revealing our needs allows others the

---

3. Bonhoeffer, p. 20.

opportunity to meet that need. It provides an opportunity for the Body to work together and for our sisters to utilize their God-given gifts to serve one another.

Lastly, this also means we can't cling tightly to our worldly goods and think that they are ours alone. All good things we have are given to us by the Lord; we are merely stewards of them. There are times when God calls us to share those blessings with others. When that happens, we need to be generous and open handed because Christ has been so generous to us. Such actions reflect and are evidence of the faith at work within us, 'If a brother or sister is poorly clothed and lacking in daily food, and one of you says to them, "Go in peace, be warmed and filled," without giving them the things needed for the body, what good is that?' (James 2:15-16).

Questions to Consider:

Read Matthew 25:31-46. What does the parable teach about who we are serving when we help someone else who is in need?

Who in your church community is struggling right now with a physical need? How could you reach out to them and offer help?

What skills do you have that you can share with someone else? Can you sew, do household repairs, cook a meal, do yard work, tutor a child in math? We all have skills we can offer a friend in need. Consider some practical ways you can do so today.

What keeps you from telling others in your church about your physical needs? How does knowing that God is loving and helping you through other people change your hesitation?

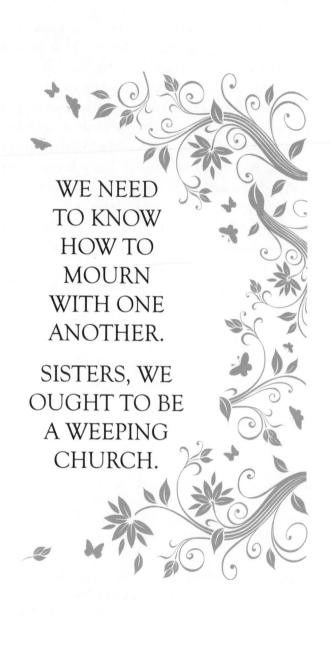

WE NEED
TO KNOW
HOW TO
MOURN
WITH ONE
ANOTHER.

SISTERS, WE
OUGHT TO BE
A WEEPING
CHURCH.

5

Sisters Mourn Together

*'I am glad you are here with me. Here at
the end of all things, Sam.'*

J. R. R. TOLKIEN [1]

I remember meeting a friend for coffee one morning. She
had just experienced a deep and painful loss in her life.
The grief was etched across her face, her eyes tired, and
her voice flat and low. As we talked, I had little to say.
Her loss was unfamiliar to me and there was little I could
add. I felt helpless. But at the same time, I knew loss in
general. I had felt that searing pain of having something
I loved ripped out of my hands. And so, I listened and
mourned with her.

---

1. Tolkein, J. R. R. *The Return of the King* (New York: Houghton Mifflin,
1995), p. 1180.

Weeping and Mourning

Because we live in a fallen world, there is much to mourn. In fact, since the advent of sin, suffering and sorrow has darkened every area of life. There is nowhere we can hide from its shadow. Illness, loss, failed dreams, rejection, abuse, and marital discord, are just a few reasons we have to mourn. Jesus warned the disciples, 'In the world you will have tribulation. But take heart; I have overcome the world' (John 16:33). The New Living Translation uses the words trials and sorrows, 'Here on earth you will have many trials and sorrows.'

Isaiah referred to our Savior as the Man of Sorrows, 'He was despised and rejected by men, a man of sorrows and acquainted with grief; and as one from whom men hide their faces he was despised, and we esteemed him not' (53:3). Indeed, Christ knew loss as He mourned at the graveside of His dear friend Lazarus. He knew rejection because those from His own hometown attempted to kill Him (Luke 4:29). He knew hunger and homelessness. He knew abandonment when His closest friends fled just when He needed them most. He knew deep sorrow as He thought about the horror that awaited Him at the cross, so much so that He cried out to His Father saying, 'Abba, Father, all things are possible for you. Remove this cup from me. Yet not what I will, but what you will' (Mark 14:36). And all of the suffering He experienced in this fallen world culminated at the cross when He felt the weight of our sin on His shoulders, 'And at the ninth hour Jesus cried with a loud voice, "Eloi, Eloi, lema sabachthani?"' which means, 'My God, my God, why have you forsaken me?' (Mark 15:34).

As followers of Christ, not only can we expect hardship, suffering, and sorrow in our life, but we are also called to walk alongside others who are suffering. In Romans 12:12, Paul tells us to 'mourn with those who mourn' (NIV). The ESV translates it as 'weep with those who weep.' The writer to the Hebrews tells us to, 'Remember those who are in prison, as though in prison with them, and those who are mistreated, since you also are in the body' (13:3). Because we are a part of the same Body, when someone is suffering, we suffer with them. In the same way that an injury to one part of our physical body affects our entire body, when one member of our church Body is hurting, we all hurt.

The book of Job tells us the story of a man who endured intense suffering. A kind of suffering most of us will never know. In the blink of an eye he lost all his children, his wealth, and his health. Job's friends came and sat with him in the customary dust and ashes that represented a person's loss and suffering. They didn't speak for seven days. 'Now when Job's three friends heard of all this evil that had come upon him, they came each from his own place, Eliphaz the Temanite, Bildad the Shuhite, and Zophar the Naamathite. They made an appointment together to come to show him sympathy and comfort him. And when they saw him from a distance, they did not recognize him. And they raised their voices and wept, and they tore their robes and sprinkled dust on their heads toward heaven. And they sat with him on the ground seven days and seven nights, and no one spoke a word to him, for they saw that his suffering was very great' (Job 2:11-13). This is what it means to mourn with those who mourn.

When we do the Opposite of Mourning

Mourning with a friend is not easy. It's hard. It's uncomfortable. It reminds us of our own suffering. It reminds us of how fleeting life is. We want their pain to go away and return to normal. We don't like the vulnerability of it all. Seeing someone weep is like seeing their soul laid out before us, naked and bare.

But we need to know how to mourn with one another. Sisters, we ought to be a weeping church. We ought to lament with one another. We ought to cry out to God in sorrow for all that our sisters are going through – for their pain is our pain.

Because we are uncomfortable with seeing someone mourn and because we often don't know what to do when someone is hurting, we often don't mourn with them. Instead we do the opposite.

We Avoid Them

When we are uncomfortable with our sister's sorrow, we avoid her. We stay away and distance ourselves. We avoid eye contact. We wait for time to pass and then expect to pick up where we left off. But avoiding our sister-friend speaks loud to her heart. It makes her think there is something wrong with her. It makes her feel isolated and alone. When she needs the love and support of her community the most and we minimize or ignore her pain altogether, we leave our sister vulnerable. We add to her already wounded heart.

We Try to Rescue Them

Sometimes we might try to save or rescue our sister from her problems. We try to take away her pain and make everything better for her. We try to solve her problems and are always ready to hand out advice. Yes, we should help our hurting sister and help in practical ways but in doing so we must do a heart check and evaluate our motives. We are not anyone's savior. As believers, we know that God often uses suffering for His redemptive purposes. So we must be watchful of our intentions – are we trying to take over and solve her problems?

Susan Hunt mentioned this desire to protect others from trials in her book, *Spiritual Mothering*. She wrote, 'I must want to help you live for God's glory. I must honestly want God's glory for your life. Now this is risky. It may well mean that the younger woman I dearly love will have to go through difficult times to be stripped of those things that hinder selfless living. I find that the more I love a younger woman, the more I want to protect and shield her. It is a constant discipline for me to stay out of the way. Encouraging and equipping is not the same as pampering and indulging. I am not to fix everything in the younger woman's life, nor am I to remove all of the tough times.'[2] We can encourage a sister without taking over and solving her problems for her. However, there are times when intervention is needed. If our sister is in physical danger, for example, we must intervene and get her help.

We Make Assumptions

Sometimes we make assumptions about why we think our friend is hurting. Remember Job's friends who sat with him

---

2. Hunt, Susan. *Spiritual Mothering: The Titus 2 Model for Women Mentoring Women* (Wheaton: Crossway, 1992), p. 132.

for seven days? Well, they should have stayed silent because after that first week they started talking and everything went downhill after that. The problem was, Job's friends did not know their theology. They believed that good behavior resulted in blessing and bad behavior resulted in punishment. That was their worldview. If you lived a good life, good things happened to you and the opposite if you did not. So when Job lost everything, they assumed that he must have disobeyed God in some profound way. Much of the book of Job documents each friend taking turns trying to get Job to admit to some kind of wrongdoing.

But Job was an upright man. He loved and served God. We know from reading Job that his suffering was not because of something he had done but because Satan came before God and said, 'Does Job fear God for no reason? Have you not put a hedge around him and his house and all that he has, on every side? You have blessed the work of his hands, and his possessions have increased in the land. But stretch out your hand and touch all that he has, and he will curse you to your face.' And the LORD said to Satan, 'Behold, all that he has is in your hand. Only against him do not stretch out your hand' (Job 1:9-12). Job's losses were not because God was punishing him for sin but because there were lessons God wanted to teach him through his suffering. There were things he needed to learn about God.

The same kind of thinking that Job's friends had still existed in Jesus' day when the disciples asked Jesus about a man born blind. They asked, 'Rabbi, who sinned, this man or his parents, that he was born blind?' (John 9:2). Jesus responded, 'It was not that this man sinned, or his parents, but that the works of God might be displayed in him' (v. 3).

This is a common error we all can make, assuming that we know why some tragedy or heartache has happened in someone's life or even trying to investigate the specific reasons why. But we can't do that; we cannot assume. Ed Welch wrote that 'such responses suggest that suffering is a solvable riddle. God has something specific in mind, and we have to guess what it is...In our attempts to help, we can over interpret suffering. We search for clues to God's ways, as if suffering were a scavenger hunt. Get to the end, with the right answers, and God will take away the pain... Suffering is not an intellectual matter that needs answers; it is highly personal.'[3]

We Speak with Platitudes

When a friend is hurting, sometimes we say unhelpful platitudes. You know what they are; we've all heard them. 'This too shall pass.' 'This will work out, things will get better. You'll see.' 'God will turn this out for your good.' 'God doesn't give you more than you can handle.' 'You should rejoice in your suffering.' These kinds of phrases remind me of the song from one of my favorite childhood movies, *Annie*: 'When I'm stuck with a day that's grey and lonely, I'll stick up my chin and grin and say...the sun will come out tomorrow.' Such phrases sound nice but hold little meaning. Sometimes they might even come from truth but are misplaced and misused.

---

3. Welch, Ed. *Side by Side: Walking With Others in Wisdom and Love* (Wheaton: Crossway, 2015), Kindle Location: 1245.

Why are such platitudes wrong to say? Ed Welch wrote that such platitudes circumvent our compassion.[4] Sometimes, even if a statement comes from Scripture, such as 'God will use this for your good' it's not the time to say it. When someone has just experienced a severe loss or some kind of tragedy, we need to be sensitive to them. When a wound is fresh, we don't want to add more pain to it. Even something that is rooted in Biblical truth like, 'You should take joy in your trials' is hurtful when someone has just learned that they have been diagnosed with stage four cancer. There is a time for speaking Biblical truths but it's not when the wound is new and raw. Also, saying something like, 'Everything is going to be ok' is unkind because it's not always true. The sun doesn't always come out tomorrow. Sometimes marriages do fail and end in divorce. People do lose their jobs and homes. The cancer doesn't always go away and people do die. As Proverbs 25:20 says, 'Whoever sings songs to a heavy heart is like one who takes off a garment on a cold day, and like vinegar on soda.' The Bible doesn't say to rejoice with those who mourn. It says to mourn with those who mourn.

All of these responses to a sister's sorrow fail to love and support her. So what should we say and do when a sister in the Lord is mourning?

Loving the Hurting

Just Listen

This is the one thing Job's friends did right. When Job suffered the tremendous loss of his family and fortune,

---

4. Welch, Kindle Location: 1234.

his friends gathered around him and didn't speak. They entered his grief and sorrow and mourned alongside him. What a hurting person needs most is just the presence of someone who loves and cares for them. Silence brings more comfort than any advice or platitude we could give. We often feel compelled to fill the empty void with words and this is our downfall. We don't have to say *anything*. If your sister in Christ wants to talk, listen to her. Look her in the eye and speak with your eyes and body language. And if you feel led, weep along with her.

As Bonhoeffer wrote, 'The first service that one owes to others in the fellowship consists in listening to them. Just as love to God begins with listening to His Word, so the beginning of love for the brethren is learning to listen to them. It is God's love for us that He not only gives us His Word but also lends us His ear. So it is His work that we do for our brother when we learn to listen to him. Christians, especially ministers, so often think they must always contribute something when they are in the company of others, that this is the one service they have to render. They forget that listening can be a greater service than speaking.'[5]

Speak Gospel Truth

We often think that the act of encouragement involves saying things that make people feel better. In *Relationships: A Mess Worth Making*, Tripp and Lane wrote, 'Encouragement is not just about making people feel and think better; it's about stimulating spiritual imagination. Encouragement

---

5. Bonhoeffer, p. 97.

gives struggling people the eyes to see an unseen Christ. He is the only reliable hope.'[6]

As we walk alongside our sister in her brokenness, there will come a time when she is ready to talk about her suffering. She will want to share the thoughts, feelings, and questions that have plagued her since the trial began. When that time comes, we need to speak to her gospel truth. We need to point her to Christ.

Encourage her with the love Jesus has for her. Remind her that God has not abandoned her and that He is her refuge and strength. Point her to the Man of Sorrows who was well acquainted with grief. Our Savior knew the sting of rejection. He knew temptation, loss, sorrow, and heartache. Jesus came to bear all our sorrows and griefs; our sin and shame. Our Savior endured more heartache and pain than we could ever imagine. He did not deserve it but endured it out of love for us. He now lives and reigns, interceding for us. Remind her of this truth. Remind her of who she is in Christ and because of Christ.

We must remember this important truth: things might not get better. Our sister in Christ may suffer from now until Christ returns or she goes home to heaven. This is why speaking gospel truth is so important. We might be tempted to say something like, 'Everything will be ok' but that doesn't give her real hope. Hope doesn't come from some cliché; it comes in the form of a person, Jesus Christ. This is the same hope that Job had when he said, 'For I know that my Redeemer lives, and at the last he will stand upon the earth' (Job 19:25). This hope is a present

---

6. Lane and Tripp, p.113.

reality as Christ lives within us and strengthens us with His grace. It is also a future reality as we look to eternity when all pain and suffering will be no more.

One of the ways you can do this practically is to invite her to read Scripture or a Christ-centered book with you. Meet regularly to talk and pray through what she is reading and learning.

Pray for Your Sister

A couple of years ago, I was at the hospital visiting a relative who was seriously ill. I looked up from my spot in the waiting room and saw a family member standing at the nurse's station, noticeably distraught and upset. I jumped up from my seat and went over to see what happened. I learned from the nurse and then confirmed with the doctor that the news for my ailing relative was grim. I didn't know what to do or say or how to help so I put my arm around my grieving family member and said, 'Let's go pray.' We found the hospital's chapel and sat down before the Lord, laying our hurts and cares before Him.

Sometimes we view prayer as one of the last things we do. When we can't think of anything else to do or say, we say 'I'll pray for you.' But in truth, prayer should be the first thing we do. Prayer is a powerful tool for the Christian. God uses our prayers to carry out His will. It's one of the weapons in our arsenal against evil spiritual forces. It brings God into our conversation. It's a way to remind our sister that God is present and that He hears her heart.

As we pray, we can pray for whatever her particular needs are (a job, for wisdom, for relief from pain), but we can also pray for her faith and that God would work in her spiritually through this trial to draw her closer to Him and make her more like Christ.

A lament is a form of prayer and we can cry out loud in lament to our Father in heaven who catches our tears in a bottle (Ps. 56:80). The Psalms contain many laments after which we can model our own prayers. The psalmist engaged God, cried out to Him, and gave voice to all his painful emotions. He asked God, 'Why?' and 'How long?' He asked God to intervene in his sorrow and sought after His help and salvation. As he prayed, he reminded himself of God's goodness and faithfulness. These are all things we can do in our own prayers for our sister who mourns.

The God of All Comfort

Paul wrote to the Corinthian church:

Blessed be the God and Father of our Lord Jesus Christ, the Father of mercies and God of all comfort, who comforts us in all our affliction, so that we may be able to comfort those who are in any affliction, with the comfort with which we ourselves are comforted by God. For as we share abundantly in Christ's sufferings, so through Christ we share abundantly in comfort too. If we are afflicted, it is for your comfort and salvation; and if we are comforted, it is for your comfort, which you experience when you patiently endure the same sufferings that we suffer. Our hope for you is unshaken, for we know that as you share in our sufferings, you will also share in our comfort. For we do not want you to be unaware, brothers, of the affliction we experienced in Asia. For we were so utterly burdened beyond our strength that we despaired of life itself. Indeed, we felt that we had received the sentence of death. But that was to make us rely not on ourselves but on God who raises the dead. He delivered us from such a deadly peril, and he will deliver us. On him we have set our hope that he will deliver us again. You also must help us by prayer, so that many will give thanks on our behalf for the blessing granted us through the prayers of many (2 Cor. 1:3-11).

This passage reminds us of our unity in Christ. Because we are united to the Vine, we receive our comfort from Him. We in turn comfort others with the same comfort God provided. We share in the sufferings of Christ and in the sufferings of other believers. *'For as we share abundantly in Christ's sufferings, so through Christ we share abundantly in comfort too. If we are afflicted, it is for your comfort and salvation; and if we are comforted, it is for your comfort, which you experience when you patiently endure the same sufferings that we suffer'* (v. 5). As the Gospel Transformation Bible notes, 'our afflictions can serve as windows to the reality and benefits of our union with Christ.'[7]

Paul was open and honest with the Corinthians about how much he suffered. 'We despaired of life itself.' He shared the depth of his sufferings with the Corinthians and he shared how God delivered him. He even revealed the spiritual lesson he learned from his trials, 'But that was to make us rely not on ourselves but on God who raises the dead' (v. 9). We comfort one another in our trials when we speak gospel truth, passing on the lessons we have learned from Christ in our own trials.

Paul then asked the Corinthians for help in prayer. By uniting together as a Body to pray for Paul, that prayer would not only help bring about God's will in Paul's life but it would also produce the fruit of thanksgiving in others (v. 11).

---

7. *Gospel Transformation Bible* (Wheaton, IL: Crossway, 2013), p. 1555.

This is the Body of Christ in action.

I can't number the times I have listened to other friends share stories of how God worked in their life and it challenged and strengthened my own faith. When I've struggled with a hardship and a friend who had already journeyed through a similar trial testified of God's goodness and loving kindness in their life, it encouraged me in my hardship. God doesn't want us to keep His comfort for ourselves, but to share that comfort with others.

Questions to Consider:

Think back to a time when you were mourning a loss or heartache of some kind. Who sat in the dust and ashes with you? What helped you the most? Think also of a time when someone was not helpful. What specific thing did that person do, not do, say, or not say that was not helpful? What can you learn from those experiences that can help you when you mourn with another sister-friend who is mourning or suffering in some way?

Though friends we have through online connections in social media can write comforting things to us when we are suffering, what are some specific ways these 'friendships' cannot mourn with us the way a sister in our church can?

Read Isaiah 61. Jesus read this passage in the synagogue and applied it to himself. What does it say about our Savior?

One of the reasons I wanted to write this book was to encourage us as believers to develop deep sister-friendships in the Lord so that we would have people to turn to when life gets hard. We are all walking the same journey and we can't walk it alone. Consider, who are those people? Who can you turn to when you are weeping? Who can you call to come and pray with you?

AS WE SEEK
TO FIND OUR
CONTENTMENT
IN CHRIST,
OUR SISTER'S
JOY BECOMES
OUR JOY.

6

Sisters Rejoice Together

*'True love will interest us in the sorrows
and joys of one another, and teach us to
make them our own.'*

MATTHEW HENRY[1]

IN our last house, we had a large screened-in back porch. It was host to numerous celebrations over the years. We held baby and adoption showers for friends. We had birthday parties, not just for our family but for friends as well. We said farewell to friends at going away parties. We filled that slab of concrete full of church family to rejoice and celebrate God's goodness in one another's lives.

On the whole, we do a great job in our churches celebrating with one another. We throw bridal showers for

---

1. Henry, Matthew. *Matthew Henry's Commentary on the Whole Bible* (Peabody, Massachusetts: Hendrickson Publishers, 1991), p. 2228.

young brides. We host baby showers for expectant moms. We announce momentous anniversaries. We attend each other's birthday celebrations, graduation parties, and housewarmings. There is no doubt; church members enjoy celebrating special occasions with one another.

Rejoice with One Another

In the book of Romans, Paul wrote to the Roman church a rather lengthy and theologically rich letter. He unpacked the gospel in great detail, helping them understand their absolute depravity, God's absolute righteousness, and the righteousness that was theirs through faith in Christ. In the last few chapters of Romans, Paul turned to the practical application of how the gospel applied to the Christian life and what it looks like to live as a Christian. Because they were now righteous in Christ, these Roman believers could now live in righteousness. In the middle of Romans 12, Paul gave a list of specific actions for Christians, many of which related to how they were to interact with one another.

In the previous chapter, we looked at half of Romans 12:15 'mourn with those who mourn.' The other half is this: 'rejoice with those who rejoice.' When someone has reason to give thanks to God, we are to join them, giving thanks alongside them. In 1 Corinthians 12:26, Paul wrote something similar to the Corinthian church, 'If one member suffers, all suffer together; if one member is honored, all rejoice together.' This instruction alludes again to our unity in the Body of Christ.

At first glance, such an instruction seems simple. It means we buy shower gifts and sing 'Happy Birthday.' Right? Yes, but I think it means more. It means that we ought to have joy for what God is doing in the life of our sister in the Lord. Yet sometimes, such joy is hard, especially when the blessing in our sister's life reminds us of the blessing we think is missing in our life.

Begrudging our Sisters

When God provides for a sister in Christ, answers her prayer, or blesses her in some way, our first response is not always to rejoice. Imagine with me if you will, a sister-friend who announces her pregnancy. You've struggled for months to get pregnant. Is your first response to her news to rejoice? Or do you look at her growing belly with bitterness? What about a sister who invites you to a house warming party at the home she's just moved into. You walk into the house and it's bigger than yours, has an amazing layout, and is in the exact location you've always wanted to live. Does your heart rejoice with her at what God has provided? What if you are always the bridesmaid and never the bride? Or what if your friend's child gets into the college of their choice while your child barely got into the local community college? What if a sister-friend's child excels in sports and your child can hardly run without tripping over themselves? Can you be glad for her?

There are countless scenarios where our sisters in the Lord might be blessed and we might struggle to rejoice with them. We may attend the showers. We might sign the birthday or anniversary cards. We might smile at their good news. But inside, in the depths of our heart, we shout, 'It's not fair! Why her and not me?' Deep inside we begrudge our sisters. We do not rejoice at what God is doing. We compare our life to her life. We look at the story God is writing in her life and we desire it for ourselves.

Begrudging a sister in the Lord is not a new sin. It's a sin we all battle. It's a sin that keeps us from rejoicing with those who rejoice. It keeps us from living out our unity in Christ.

After Moses delivered the Israelites from Pharaoh and brought them out into the desert to begin their long trek to the Promised Land, God met with Moses on Mount Sinai to give him the law. Israel was God's people, God's community, and they had to learn what it looked like to live in community with one another. They had been living in a land where people worshipped everything but the one true God. They needed to learn who God is and what He expected from them.

God scratched into stone the Ten Commandments. He began the list by instructing His people to love, serve, and worship Him alone. 'You shall have no other gods before me. You shall not make for yourself an image in the form of anything in heaven above or on the earth beneath or in the waters below. You shall not bow down to them or worship them; for I, the Lord your God, am a jealous God, punishing the children for the sin of the parents to the third and fourth generation of those who hate me, but showing love to a thousand generations of those who love me and keep my commandments' (Exod. 20:3-6). After seven other commands, He added a bookend, 'You shall not covet your neighbor's house; you shall not covet your neighbor's wife, or his male servant, or his female servant, or his ox, or his donkey, or anything that is your neighbor's' (Exod. 20:17). To covet is to desire something that is not yours. It is to look at what someone else has and want it for yourself. Such desire says in effect, 'What God has given me is not enough. I need more.' In fact, to covet is to do the opposite of the first commandment. It is to put something on the altar of our heart and honor and worship it, taking a place that belongs to God alone. To covet is to worship.

Another word for covet is envy. Jonathan Edwards defined envy as 'a spirit of dissatisfaction with, and opposition to, the prosperity and happiness of others as compared with our own…when we dislike and are opposed to another's honor or prosperity, because, in general, it is greater than our own, or because, in particular, they have some honor or enjoyment that we have not.'[2] This same covetousness or envy ate at the heart of David when he looked out from his castle balcony and saw Bathsheba, 'It happened, late one afternoon, when David arose from his couch and was walking on the roof of the king's house, that he saw from the roof a woman bathing; and the woman was very beautiful' (2 Sam. 11:2). He learned from a servant that she was Uriah's wife. And then he took her for himself. Following his sin, he attempted to cover it up by placing her husband at the front of the battle so that he would die, leaving Bathsheba free to be his.

Envy is a disordered desire. James says that our envy and our disordered desires affect our relationships with one another, 'What causes quarrels and what causes fights among you? Is it not this, that your passions are at war within you? You desire and do not have, so you murder.

---

2. Edwards, p. 71.

You covet and cannot obtain, so you fight and quarrel. You do not have, because you do not ask. You ask and do not receive, because you ask wrongly, to spend it on your passions' (4:1-3).

Such envy is listed in the famous love chapter, 1 Corinthians 13, 'Love is patient and kind; *love does not envy* (emphasis mine) or boast; it is not arrogant or rude. It does not insist on its own way; it is not irritable or resentful; it does not rejoice at wrongdoing, but rejoices with the truth. Love bears all things, believes all things, hopes all things, endures all things' (vv. 4-7). One of the defining characteristics of love is that it does not envy. As we've seen in an earlier chapter, love is one of the marks of a Christian. The love that believers have for one another is a testimony of Christ to the watching world. When we envy our sister-friends, we have not love, and we fail to shine a light, pointing to Christ as Lord to those around us.

For those of us who envy and fail to rejoice with others, there is good news.

A Sympathetic High Priest

Before Jesus began His ministry, He wandered in the wilderness (Matt. 4). For forty days He was without food. He was weak, empty, and hungry to be filled. Satan found Jesus in this weakened state and stepped in to tempt Him, offering Him everything on a silver platter, if only He would disobey God and serve him. 'Again, the devil took him to a very high mountain and showed him all the kingdoms of the world and their glory. And he said to him, "All these I will give you, if you will fall down and worship me"' (vv. 8-9). But Christ, being fully God, did not sin.

He faced temptation and conquered it with the word of God. 'Then Jesus said to him, "Be gone, Satan! For it is written, 'You shall worship the Lord your God and him only shall you serve'"' (v. 10). Jesus did what the Israelites could not do during their desert wanderings; He loved and worshipped God alone. Jesus did what **we** cannot do; He loved and worshipped God alone.

Because of Jesus, because of His perfect life lived on our behalf, His triumph over temptation becomes ours. We can face our inordinate desires, our envy, our coveting, with the knowledge that Christ has won the battle for us. He has defeated sin and death. He has given us a new heart to love God alone. These are gospel truths we must remember when we battle against envy in our heart.

The gospel also reminds us that God does not begrudge us. 'He has not begrudged us his only-begotten and well-beloved Son, who was dearer to him than everything beside, nor hath he begrudged us the highest honor and blessedness in and through him.'[3] God has held nothing back. He has not treated us as our sins deserve and has instead showered us with grace upon grace. He provides us life, breath, and everything else. He strengthens and sustains us. He gives us every spiritual blessing in Christ.

So when we are tempted to envy our sisters, we can remember Jesus and what He has done. 'For we do not have a high priest who is unable to sympathize with our weaknesses, but one who in every respect has been tempted as we are, yet without sin' (Heb. 4:15). We can repent of our sin and receive the cleansing forgiveness Jesus provided

---

3. Edwards, p. 75.

through the gospel. Then strengthened by His grace, we can turn away from our envy and rejoice in what God is doing in the lives of others.

Contentment in Christ

At the core of our envy is seeking contentment everywhere else but in Christ. When our sister-friend rejoices over a job offer or when she is honored before others for her work in ministry or when a dream she has long held has been fulfilled and we look at what she has and think, 'My life would be better if I had what she has' we are seeking our contentment outside of Christ. As redeemed saints and children of the living God, we are to find our contentment in who we are in Christ, not what we have or do not have.

The Apostle Paul informed the Philippians in his letter to them that he knew the secret to contentment. They wanted to provide for some of his needs. In a section of his letter where he thanked them for their contribution, he shared with them that after experiencing times in his life when he had plenty and times when he had nothing, he had learned how to be content no matter his circumstance, 'Not that I am speaking of being in need, for I have learned in whatever situation I am to be content. I know how to be brought low, and I know how to abound. In any and every circumstance, I have learned the secret of facing plenty and hunger, abundance and need. I can do all things through him who strengthens me' (4:11-13).

Like Paul, our own contentment needs to be rooted in Christ, who He is, what He has done, and who we are because of it. In Christ, we have all we need or could ever desire. In Him, we find our meaning and purpose. We find our identity as those who have been rescued from sin and adopted into the family of God.

Finding our meaning in Christ keeps us focused on the work He has for us rather than what He is doing in the lives of others. Instead of comparing our story to someone else's, we joyfully live out the one God wrote for us. We won't live our life dependent on a change in circumstances but will trust in the knowledge that everything God places in our life is for His glory and our ultimate good.

There may be times when our sister's joy reminds us of our deep sorrows. We can't help it – her joy pricks at our loss. In our sadness, we can turn to Christ, bring Him our sorrows, and find comfort in Him. We can rest in His strength and care for us. We can fellowship with Him in our sufferings, remembering His suffering for us. As we do, we'll find that Christ is our hope. And though our heart still sighs, we can rejoice alongside our sister, knowing that Christ carries our burdens. 'Surely he has borne our griefs and carried our sorrows' (Isa. 53:4).

Their Joy is Our Joy

As we seek to find our contentment in Christ, our sister's joy becomes our joy. We won't hear her good news and envy what God has done, instead we will rejoice with all our heart. For we know that she is united to us as we are united to Christ. The good that happens in her life is also our good and vice versa.

As John Calvin wrote in his commentary on Romans 12, '...the faithful, regarding each other with mutual affection, are to consider the condition of others as their own...they were to "rejoice with the joyful, and to weep with the weeping." For such is the nature of true love, that one prefers to weep with his brother, rather than to look at a distance on his grief, and to live in pleasure or ease. What is meant then is, – that we, as much as possible, ought to sympathize with one another, and that, whatever our lot may be, each should transfer to himself the feeling of another, whether of grief in adversity, or of joy in prosperity. And, doubtless, not to regard with joy the happiness of a brother is envy; and not to grieve for his misfortunes is inhumanity. Let there be such a sympathy among us as may at the same time adapt us to all kinds of feelings.'[4]

In fact, we should go beyond merely rejoicing with our sisters. As Paul also wrote in Romans 12, 'Love one another with brotherly affection. Outdo one another in showing honor' (v. 10). We should brag about our sisters in the Lord. We should go out of our way to show honor. We should not only attend a wedding shower but be the one that throws it. We should share their good news with others as though it is our good news. Because the truth is, it is.

Questions to Consider:

What ways might you begrudge another sister? How does remembering your unity in Christ change your envy toward her?

Read James 4:7-10. What does James say to do when we covet?

Consider specific ways you could rejoice for and honor another sister-friend.

4. Calvin, John. *Commentary on Romans.* www.ccel.org/ccel/calvin/cal-com38.xvi.v.html. Accessed 8/27/2016.

WE CAN'T
JOURNEY
TOGETHER
IN THE FAITH
IF WE ARE
NOT OPEN
ABOUT OUR
HARDSHIPS,
TRIALS, AND
SINS.

7

Sisters Exhort One Another

'But thank you most of all for friends. We appreciate the complicated and wonderful gifts you give us in each other. And we appreciate the task you put down before us, of loving each other the best we can, even as you love us. We pray in Christ's name, Amen.'

KATE DICAMILLO [1]

ABOUT five years ago, the company my husband worked for gave him a trip as a gift for working there ten years. We could go anywhere we wanted. It happened to be our

---

1. DiCamillo, Kate. *Because of Winn Dixie* (Somerville, MA: Candlewick Press, 2000), p. 153.

fifteenth wedding anniversary so we chose to go to Paris, France. As we prepared for our trip, I wondered what I would wear. My South Florida wardrobe consisted mostly of flip-flops, tees, and shorts. Not exactly Paris couture. So I enlisted the help of friends I considered more stylish than I.

I ended up with multiple outfits in varying shades of grey and black. And scarves. Lots of scarves. The trouble was, when I put them on, something felt wrong. I didn't look or feel like myself. It felt more like I was playing dress up. It was like being a preschooler again, putting on discarded grownup clothes: dresses that cascaded and dragged beyond my feet, shoes that flopped as I walked, and big chunky necklaces that got caught up around my elbows. Wearing such clothes made me feel like a pretender. It was like wearing an Ancient Greek actor's mask and pretending to be someone else altogether.

Pretending No More

In the church, pretending comes naturally. Rather than feel uncomfortable, we are so used to our masks and disguises that the persona we wear is more familiar than what lies underneath. The pretending we do in the church doesn't involve playing dress up or wearing real masks. But we pretend nonetheless.

How do we pretend? We put on our very best each Sunday morning and respond to each greeting of 'How are you?' with a smile, a nod, and an 'I am well. How are you?' in return. When in reality, we had one of the worst weeks of our lives. We pretend that life is going smoothly when it is not. We pretend that we have it altogether when we don't. We pretend that we have no struggles, no temptations, and no sorrows.

When it's our turn to offer up prayer needs at Bible study, we request prayer for our child's health or behavior and never share that we are at our wit's end in our parenting. When a wise older sister looks us in the eye and asks how we are really doing, we say we are tired and stressed but fail to mention that our marriage is splintering and we wonder if God even cares. Or we slink into church late every Sunday and leave before the last hymn so no one gets the chance to see our eyes swollen from all the tears we've cried.

In all our pretending, we've told ourselves a lie that everyone has it together except for us. We've convinced ourselves that no one would understand what we are going through. We fear judgment, pity, and shocked faces if anyone knew just how much we struggled. The risk is too high to let our guard down, to stop pretending and let someone know what really lies behind our masks.

The truth is, as sisters united in Christ, we all come to faith the same way – by grace through faith. We are all sinners in need of a Savior. Not one of us has an advantage over another. We are all lost, alone, orphaned, and broken. Some have described the church as not a museum of saints but a hospital for sinners. And we are all sick.

Therefore, since we are all broken sinners in need of salvation, why do we pretend otherwise? Why do we pretend that we have no sin? Why do we pretend that we have it altogether and that we have no doubts, struggles, temptations, or trials? Why do we pretend that our quiet times are always fruitful, that our marriage is thriving, that we have no fears?

The Apostle Paul, the one who had every reason to boast (2 Cor. 11), shared with the Corinthian church how overwhelmed and crushed he felt during his experiences in Asia. 'For we do not want you to be unaware, brothers, of the affliction we experienced in Asia. For we were so utterly burdened beyond our strength that we despaired of life itself' (2 Cor. 1:8). Later, in chapter seven, he told them of his fears, 'For even when we came into Macedonia, our bodies had no rest, but we were afflicted at every turn – fighting without and fear within' (v. 5). These are honest statements – from one whom we might think at first glance had it altogether – shared with his fellow brothers and sisters in the Lord.

Sisters, we must be believers who are honest with one another. We can't journey together in the faith if we are not open about our hardships, trials, and sins. We can't fulfill many of the admonitions in Scripture, if we don't know what is going on in each other's lives. How can we 'bear one another's burdens' (Gal. 6:2) if we don't know each other's burdens? How can we 'encourage one another and build one another up' (1 Thess. 5:11) if we don't know that our sister is discouraged and needs building up? How can we mourn with those who mourn if we don't know that our sister has reason to mourn?

Even our Savior sought the fellowship of His brothers Peter, James, and John when He went to the Father in prayer the evening of His arrest. He was in great despair over what He knew was to come and asked them to help Him by watching and praying. 'And they went to a place called Gethsemane. And he said to his disciples, "Sit here while I pray." And he took with him Peter and James and

John, and began to be greatly distressed and troubled. And he said to them, "My soul is very sorrowful, even to death. Remain here and watch." And going a little farther, he fell on the ground and prayed that, if it were possible, the hour might pass from him. And he said, "Abba, Father, all things are possible for you. Remove this cup from me. Yet not what I will, but what you will." And he came and found them sleeping, and he said to Peter, "Simon, are you asleep? Could you not watch one hour? Watch and pray…"' (Mark 14:32-38). If our Savior needed community at His darkest hour, why would we be ashamed to share our own needs and sorrows with others in our community?

Will you join me in removing your mask and stop pretending?

Being Real with One Another

About ten years ago, I met with the pastor of my church to talk about women's ministry and my place in it. My intention in meeting with him was to share my spiritual needs in the hopes that the women's ministry could meet those needs. I hoped that there would be some sort of Bible study I could join that would feed me in the way I perceived I needed.

Instead, my pastor encouraged me to meet with a group of other women for the purpose of prayer, accountability, and discipleship. It wasn't the response I expected but it was just what I needed. I left that meeting and reached out to a group of women in my church and for the next five years we met weekly in my home. We read together, prayed together, encouraged one another, exhorted one another, and preached the gospel to each other. We kept each other accountable in areas of our faith where we were weak, with temptations we faced, and in areas of sin we battled.

Hebrews 3:13 says, 'But exhort one another every day, as long as it is called "today," that none of you may be hardened by the deceitfulness of sin.' Matthew Henry, in his commentary on Hebrews reminds us that we need each other to fight against sin, 'Since to-morrow is not ours, we must make the best improvement of this day. And there are none, even the strongest of the flock, who do not need help of other Christians. Neither are there any so low and despised, but the care of their standing in the faith, and of their safety, belongs to all.'[2]

Have you ever walked around all day with spinach stuck between your teeth or maybe your hair was matted by something sticky? Or perhaps left the house with something about your outfit wrong, maybe a tag sticking out? And then a friend quietly points to your teeth and whispers the ugly truth. It's embarrassing when we learn that food has been in our teeth all day, but we are thankful to our friend for telling us. It is one thing to see the spinach in our teeth that we don't realize is there; it's another for a friend to point out the things in ourselves that we can't see – the spiritual things. Sin is deceitful and blinds us to the truth so we need others who will point out that truth to us. A sister-friend in the Lord who spots sin in our life and exhorts us to turn back to God is a good friend. As Spurgeon noted, 'But true friends put enough trust in you to tell you openly of your faults. Give me for a friend the

---

2. Henry, p. 2385.

man who will speak honestly of me before my face; who will not tell first one neighbor, and then another, but who will come straight to my house, and say, "Sir, I feel there is such-and-such a thing in you, which, as my brother, I must tell you of." That man is a true friend; he has proved himself to be so; for we never get any praise for telling people of their faults; we rather hazard their dislike; a man will sometimes thank you for it, but he does not often like you any the better.'[3]

The Psalmist wrote, 'Let a righteous man strike me – it is a kindness; let him rebuke me – it is oil for my head; let my head not refuse it' (141:5). Proverbs 27:6 says, 'Faithful are the wounds of a friend.' Such exhorting is painful. No one likes light to shine on the darkness of their heart. But it is important and necessary.

An exhorting relationship is a relationship that sharpens. 'As iron sharpens iron, so a friend sharpens a friend' (Prov. 27:17 NLT). In metallurgy, to sharpen something is to grind away material on a tool with another abrasive material that is harder than the tool being sharpened. So a friend that is wiser in an area of Scripture sharpens us by pointing out to us how God's word applies to a particular situation in our life. This is similar to the passage in Hebrews that says, 'And let us consider how to stir up one another to love and good works' (Heb. 10:24). The remarkable thing about this process is not only does the one sharpened change by the sharpening but the one doing the sharpening changes as well. Consider how often

---

3. Spurgeon, Charles 'A Faithful Friend' (Sermon 120) www.spurgeon. org/sermons/0120.php. Accessed 10/21/16.

you have grown in times when you have taught someone else truth from God's word.

Dietrich Bonhoeffer believed that exhorting one another with the truth of God's word is a ministry of mercy, an offer of genuine fellowship. 'The basis upon which Christians can speak to one another is that each knows the other as a sinner, who, with all his human dignity, is lonely and lost if he is not given help. This is not to make him contemptible nor to disparage him in any way. On the contrary, it is to accord him the one real dignity that man has, namely, that, though he is a sinner, he can share in God's grace and glory and be God's child. This recognition gives to our brotherly speech the freedom and candor that it needs. We speak to one another on the basis of the help we both need. We admonish one another to go the way that Christ bids us to go. We warn one another against the disobedience that is our common destruction.'[4]

A friendship with other sisters in the Lord that includes accountability and exhortation is not a relationship where we simply sit around and point fingers at one another. It's not an opportunity to make people feel bad. It's not an opportunity for judgementalism where we relish pointing out the faults in another. Rather, it's a relationship where we grieve to see another sister stumble in sin. Because we are united to one another, it hurts the Body when one part turns away from God to do their own thing. The efforts we make to exhort one another or hold one another accountable are always done out of love and gentleness. 'A word fitly spoken is like apples of gold in a setting of silver. Like

4. Bonhoeffer, pp. 105-106.

a gold ring or an ornament of gold is a wise reprover to a listening ear' (Prov. 25:11-12). We go out of our way to speak to them in kindness, encouraging them, and seeking to spur them on forward in the faith. As the Apostle Paul wrote to the Galatians, 'Brothers, if anyone is caught in any transgression, you who are spiritual should restore him in a spirit of gentleness. Keep watch on yourself, lest you too be tempted' (6:1).

We see the quicksand they are stepping into and we desperately want to pull them out before it sucks them in. So we preach the gospel to them. We remind them of who they are in Christ and what He has done for them. We remind them they were bought at a price, they are new creations, and Christ will not forsake them. We point them to the cross, to redemption, forgiveness, and the way of repentance. And we offer to walk with them in the journey.

Because the truth is, Christ died not only to free us from sin but also for our sanctification. He delivered us so that we would be freed to live in righteousness. 'He himself bore our sins in his body on the tree, that we might die to sin and live to righteousness. By his wounds you have been healed' (1 Pet. 2:24). Christ cares about our holiness. He desires that we be transformed and changed into His likeness. One of the ways He pushes forward our transformation is through other believers encouraging, challenging, spurring, and exhorting us.

Yet not only do sisters in the Lord point out sins we might not notice, but we also mutually confess our sins to each other, not because we have the power to forgive sin – God alone can – but because we don't want secrets. We want the truth brought out of darkness and into the light where it loses its power. Sin likes to stay hidden but the more it's brought out into the light and the more we share it with others, the less power it holds.

In our mutual confession, there is mutual humility. We know the truth about the condition of our hearts and our great need for a Savior. 'All we like sheep have gone astray; we have turned – every one – to his own way; and the LORD has laid on him the iniquity of us all' (Isa. 53:6). We are all a work in progress; the Spirit is refining and transforming each one of us. Though we each struggle in differing ways, we all battle against sin. So when a sister reveals she is fighting against the sin of anger, materialism, immoral sexual fantasies or behaviors, envy, substance abuse, or any other sin, we listen to her in all humility because we know that our sins are just as heinous and also need the cleansing blood of Christ.

Therefore, we ask each other to pray for our sins and temptations. As James wrote, such prayer is powerful, 'Therefore, confess your sins to one another and pray for one another, that you may be healed. The prayer of a righteous person has great power as it is working' (5:16). We pray for the Spirit's work in each other's lives, for the gospel to grow bigger and brighter, and that we would all know more and more of Christ's great love for us. We pray for our sisters the way Paul prayed for the church in Colossae, 'And so, from the day we heard, we have not ceased to pray for you, asking that you may be filled with the knowledge of his will in all spiritual wisdom and understanding, so as to walk in a manner worthy of the Lord, fully pleasing to him: bearing fruit in every good work and increasing in the knowledge of God; being strengthened with all power, according to his glorious might, for all endurance and patience with joy; giving thanks to the Father, who has qualified you to share in the inheritance of the saints in light' (1:9-12).

A relationship where sisters hold each other accountable, where we gently point out sin, and where we encourage one another in the gospel, is a mutual one. It is built on trust and involves that giving and taking we talked about earlier. We exhort our sister when she is in a season of battling temptation and then she in turn does the same for us. Such trust is what I want to address next.

A Question of Trust

Whenever I have written on this topic before, readers have written and asked me, 'Do you mean we are supposed to be this way with everyone in the church?' They wonder if they are supposed to be honest, real, and transparent with everyone they meet on Sunday morning. No, I don't mean that.

When we gather in church on the Lord's Day, the people we see lining the pews are what theologians call the 'visible church.' Some of these people are members of the church and have professed Christ. Others are visitors. Still others come and go and are generally non-committal. Still others think they know what it means to be a Christian but have never understood the gospel of grace.

Within that gathered crowd are members of the 'invisible church.' These are people who have been chosen before the foundation of the world to be holy and blameless. They are the ones for whom Christ died particularly. These are the brothers and sisters we will spend thousands and thousands

115

of years singing praises alongside in the New Jerusalem. God alone knows His children; He alone knows who is in the invisible church.

So, no, I would not walk up to anyone who attends church on a Sunday morning and share with them your deepest struggles and pains. It takes time to identify people who are trustworthy, people with whom we can be vulnerable and real. As Spurgeon suggested, 'do not write "friend" yet; wait a wee bit, until you know more of him; just see him, examine him, try him, test him, and not till then enter him on the sacred list of friends. Be friendly to all, but make none your friends until they know you, and you know them. Many a friendship born in the darkness of ignorance, hath died suddenly in the light of a better acquaintance with each other.'[5]

Trustworthy friendship develops through a process which begins with simple friendship where we bond with another person over common likes and interests. Over time the friendship develops into one where we can trust each other and mutually share our burdens. Even in the group I mentioned earlier in this chapter, it took time for us to come to a place where we could be open with one another about our deep heart struggles. At first, our prayer requests were for practical things, such as God's provision or the health of our children. Over time, as people began to feel comfortable with one another, we shared deeper struggles and asked one another for prayer in areas of sin and spiritual growth.

For some of us, this is easier to do than for others. Those who have been deeply hurt in the past have a harder time revealing their wounds, struggles, sins, and temptations than

5. Spurgeon, Accessed 10/21/16.

others do, and for good reason. I have had several friends over the years who have shared with me painful stories about their lives in increments, slowly over a period of time. It took quite a while before I learned the true depths of the trauma or sorrow or brokenness they had experienced in life. But I had to show myself as trustworthy, that I wouldn't turn my back on them, use the information against them, or broadcast it to anyone else.

But it is important that we have at least a few people in our local church with whom we have an honest relationship. We need to have sister-friends whom we can ask for prayer about sins and temptations in our life. Later in the book I will talk more about pursuing such relationships, but for now, I wanted to clarify that we can't have these types of relationships with every single person in our church. To be honest, there are people in the church who are not trustworthy. There are people with whom we should be cautious because they are gossips or don't understand the gospel of grace or are manipulators or who delight to look down on others. Remember that even in the twelve, there resided a Judas Iscariot. We ought to be prayerful, asking the Lord to bring people in our lives with whom we can have a sharpening, exhorting relationship. '… until we all reach unity in the faith and in the knowledge of the Son of God and become mature, attaining to the whole measure of the fullness of Christ' (Eph. 4:13).

Let me end with this quote from Paul Tripp that sums up this chapter well, 'Many believers live their lives with a huge separation between their public church personas and the details of their private existence. We are skilled at brief, nonpersonal conversations about the weather, sports, and politics. We are learned at giving either nonanswers or spiritually platitudinous answers to people's questions. We live in long-term networks of terminally casual relationships. No one really knows us beneath the well-crafted public display, and because they don't know us, they cannot minister to us, because no one can minister to that which he does not know…But the Bible is clear. When each part is working properly, the body of Christ grows to maturity in Christ. We each need to live in intentionally intrusive, Christ-centered, grace-driven redemptive community. This community is meant to enlighten and protect. It is meant to motivate and encourage. It is meant to rescue and restore… It is meant to incarnate the love and grace of Jesus when you feel discouraged and alone. It is meant to be a visible representation of the grace of Jesus that is your hope. It is not a luxury. It is a spiritual necessity.'[6]

Questions to Consider:

What is your first thought when you hear the word 'accountability' or 'exhorting one another'? Is it positive? Negative?

Why do you think God calls us to have exhorting relationships where we sharpen one another in the faith?

Do you currently have relationships where people can exhort you and spur you on in the faith? Why or why not?

Are you the kind of friend who can speak the truth in love and gentleness?

How do you think the age of social media contributes to the challenges we have in being honest with others?

---

6. Tripp, Paul. *New Morning Mercies: A Daily Gospel Devotional* (Wheaton, IL: Crossway, 2014), July 12th Devotional.

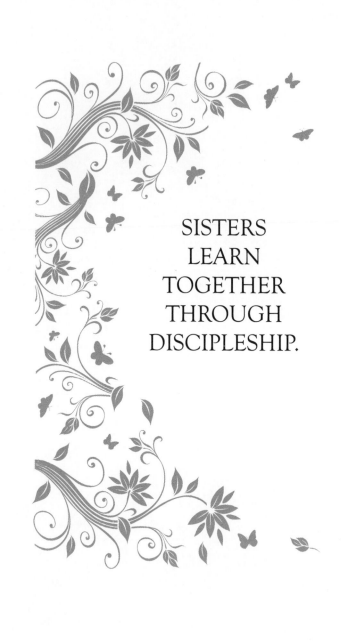

SISTERS
LEARN
TOGETHER
THROUGH
DISCIPLESHIP.

8

Sisters Learn From One Another

'...tell to the coming generation the glorious deeds of the LORD, and his might, and the wonders that he has done.'

PSALM 78:4

ONE Christmas, while visiting relatives, my husband fell and broke his ankle. We were all gathered in another room but heard the sound of the break; it seemed to echo in my ears in the silence that followed. Soon there was a flurry of activity as everyone ran to help.

The following month he ended up having surgery to repair his ankle. In the days leading up to his surgery, my older friend and leader of my discipleship group texted to ask me how my husband was doing. She asked how she could pray and, as a nurse, shared with me her knowledge about what to expect from his surgery. She knew I was nervous about it (and not good with hospitals!) and asked to join me on the day of the surgery.

That day arrived and I sat in the waiting room with my gaze fixed on the television screen that showed the progress in each step of my husband's care. Then in walked my friend. I was so thankful! She sat with me and kept me company. We had lunch together. Then we went into the hospital's chapel where we prayed for the surgery. I can't tell you how much it meant to me that my discipleship group leader would go out of her way to spend time with me at the hospital. God used her prayers to strengthen my worried heart and give me peace.

Titus 2 Discipleship

The Apostle Paul wrote a letter to Titus, the pastor of a church on the island of Crete. The island of Crete was known in the ancient world for its immorality. The church there was dealing with multiple issues, most pressing of which was the influence of false teachers. Paul doesn't describe specifically what these false teachers were teaching but he does say that they did not live in a way that proved that they knew God. He wrote in Titus 1:16, 'They profess to know God, but they deny him by their works. They are detestable, disobedient, unfit for any good work.'

Throughout the book, Paul showed Titus what a gospel-centered church looks like. He instructed Titus on how to select elders and deacons as well as the importance of preaching God's word. In Titus Chapter 2, Paul gave Titus specific instructions for various groups in the church. He explained how older and younger men, older and younger women, and slaves were to live out the gospel in their life.

In Titus 2:1-5 Paul wrote, 'But as for you, teach what accords with sound doctrine. Older men are to be sober-minded, dignified, self-controlled, sound in faith, in love, and in steadfastness. Older women likewise are to be reverent in behavior, not slanderers or slaves to much wine. They are to teach what is good, and so train the young women to love their husbands and children, to be self-controlled, pure, working at home, kind, and submissive to their own husbands, that the word of God may not be reviled.'

First, Paul instructed Titus to teach what is true and consistent with God's word. Then he gave instructions for older men. They were to be sober-minded, dignified, self-controlled, sound in faith, in love, and in steadfastness. Verse three tells us that older women were to be the same. It says 'older women likewise' were to live lives consistent with what is good. Their behavior was to be reverent, not slanderers or addicted. Then Paul instructed Titus to have these older women instruct the younger women.

They were to teach younger women what it means to love and submit to their husbands, how to glorify God in their mothering, and what it looks like to be a woman of God. These older women were to disciple younger women. They were to be spiritual mentors, in essence, spiritual mothers to these younger women.

'Older woman' is not just a reference to age. It also involves spiritual maturity. These older women Paul referred to were women who learned God's word in church and then passed on what they learned to younger women. They were mature enough in their faith to have implemented the Biblical teaching they learned in their own life. As such, they were women who lived out what they believed. They were able to model godly behavior to other women, specifically younger women.

The goal of their mentoring or discipleship was that they would shine a light in their dark world. As these younger women learned from the older women how to live out their faith, how to apply the truths of God's word to their lives, they would not 'malign the word of God.' As these women lived out their calling to be women of God, the world around them would see their life and God would be glorified.

It is important to note that these young women would not be changed or transformed by the older women. Paul wrote later in the same chapter, 'For the grace of God has appeared, bringing salvation for all people, training us to renounce ungodliness and worldly passions, and to live self-controlled, upright, and godly lives in the present age, waiting for our blessed hope, the appearing of the glory of our great God and Savior Jesus Christ, who gave himself for us to redeem us from all lawlessness and to purify for himself a people for his own possession who are zealous for good works' (2:11-14).

It is God's grace, through the power of the gospel, that trains us and changes us. So these discipleship relationships, these spiritual mentors, were conduits of God's grace. They were to point the younger women to Christ, to the truth of who God made them to be, to what it looks like to live for Christ as women. And as they taught them to apply the gospel to their lives, these women would be changed by God's grace at work in them.

Learning From One Another

Discipleship is an area of sisterhood in the church that is often neglected. When I think of the friendships I make with others in my local church Body, to be honest, I tend to connect with other women in the same age and stage of life as I am. When I was first married, I wanted to find friends who were also married without children. When I had my first son, I spent most days with other moms who also had young children. Even now, as I am new to our church, I find myself seeking friendships with those whose kids are similar in age to mine.

But in Titus 2, Paul tells us that discipleship relationships with people who are older than us are important. The Bible speaks little about women's ministry but this is one passage that addresses the need for women to disciple other women. It's not a suggestion; it's a command. Susan Hunt said this on the topic of women discipling other women, 'When we begin talking about investing in women, we're talking about this concept of the communion of the saints, that, because we're joined to Christ, we're joined to one another. We're actually obliged to share our gifts and graces – the gifts of our understandings, the gifts of our experiences, and the graces that God has worked into our lives. That's what Titus 2:3-5 is all about, sharing those gifts and graces with one another.'[1]

There is much we can learn from older women. No matter what age or stage we are in, there is always someone

---

1. Hunt, Susan. Transcript for 'Spiritual Mothering: The Titus 2 Mandate for Women Mentoring Women' October 15, 2010 www.reviveourhearts. com/events/true-woman-10-fort-worth/spiritual-mothering/transcript/. Accessed 9/11/16.

ahead of us on the journey. Those who have lived out the gospel longer than we do have wisdom and encouragement to share with us. They know the temptations we face, the sorrows of life in a fallen world, and how God works to grow our faith. They know because they have been there. They have lost babies, faced financial struggles, seen relationships crumble, journeyed through doubt, and have seen God at work time and time again. They have had to preach the gospel to themselves day in and day out. Because we are on the same path, when we look down, we can see their footprints going on ahead of us. A discipleship relationship involves an older woman showing a younger woman the way forward in faith.

Since we're sisters in Christ, I'll share something with you. I turned forty last year. It was a milestone in my life, a signpost marking middle age. It signified that I am halfway through this race of faith. With my children, I can see the teenage years coming on the horizon. An empty nest lies beyond the ridge. Beyond that are years of slowing down. I need older women in my life who have walked these seasons before me. I need older women who will journey with me into the fall and winter of my life. I need older women who can encourage me and speak truth into my life when everything seems uncertain and frightening. I need older women who can love me with gospel love, pick me up when I've fallen, and point me to the finish line where Christ my Savior stands waiting for me.

A spiritual mentor of mine once told me that she always has a spiritual mother in her life and a spiritual daughter. She was always simultaneously being discipled and discipling someone else. Just as there is always someone older than us, there is also someone younger than us as well. Just as we need to be mentored by older women, we also need to be spiritual mothers to other younger women. It's a baton that passes on from one woman to the next. The investment that an older woman makes in our life, we then take and pour out in another woman's life. Even a teen girl can disciple a middle-school-aged girl. Sisters disciple other sisters.

What is Discipleship?

The Bible doesn't contain the word 'discipleship.' It does, however, use the word 'disciple.' Jesus' followers were called disciples. 'When Jesus saw his mother and the disciple whom he loved standing nearby, he said to his mother, "Woman, behold, your son!"' (John 19:26). A disciple is essentially a follower of Christ. 'Whoever does not bear his own cross and come after me cannot be my disciple' (Luke 14:27). In the New Testament church, it was the same as being called a Christian, 'And in Antioch the disciples were first called Christians' (Acts 11:26).

Disciple is also used as a verb, as an action of making disciples. 'Go therefore and make disciples of all nations, baptizing them in the name of the Father and of the Son and of the Holy Spirit, teaching them to observe all that I have commanded you. And behold, I am with you always, to the end of the age.' (Matt. 28:19-20). This passage describes a process, going from sharing the gospel with someone, to the person making a profession of faith, to them getting baptized, to then teaching them all that Christ has commanded. It implies a long term relationship.

As believers, we are all disciples. We are Christ followers. And in terms of a relationship with other believers, we disciple people by teaching them who Christ is, what He has done, and what He has called them to be and do. Susan Hunt, who wrote the seminal work on older women mentoring younger women, likes to use the word 'spiritual mothering' to describe the discipleship relationship between an older and younger woman. Her definition of spiritual mothering is this: 'When a woman possessing faith and spiritual maturity enters into a nurturing relationship with a younger woman in order to encourage and equip her to live for God's glory.'[2]

A discipleship relationship isn't like attending Sunday school and listening to a teacher instruct you in a section of Scripture. It's not like sitting in a professor's class and taking notes. Discipleship is a life on life relationship. It is a nurturing relationship. Such a relationship is not about one person just handing out advice to others. It's not about sharing helpful tips on how to keep your house organized or how to get your child on a good sleep schedule or how to save money at the grocery store, as helpful as those tips might be. The truth is, if we just needed general tips for our life, we could go to Pinterest for that. Or if you prefer fewer words, we have Twitter for such advice. Rather, a Titus 2 discipleship relationship is about an older woman investing in your life to lead and guide you into greater holiness. Instead of passing on personal advice, it's about pointing you to the wisdom of God's word. It's about

---

2. Hunt, Susan. *Spiritual Mothering: The Titus 2 Model for Women Mentoring Women* (Chicago: Crossway, 2016), p. 36.

helping you understand your identity in Christ and what it means to be a daughter of the living God. Such a relationship is founded in, rooted in, and grounded in the word of God. Kristie Anyabwile wrote to older women, 'we need to learn to root our friendships, our counsel, our knowledge, and our womanhood in the finished work of Christ on our behalf. Christ did what we could not do for ourselves. Our efforts cannot earn us any merit before him. You can add balance to our expectations, pointing us to Christ and reminding us that our hope is in him.'[3]

As Susan Hunt's definition of spiritual mothering or Titus 2 discipleship reveals, a discipleship relationship involves encouraging and equipping. You can't have one without the other. To have equipping all on its own would be more like attending a seminar or class. It is detached and not relational. Discipleship is equipping through relationships.

We all know what it is like to be encouraged. When someone builds us up with their words, and honors us by saying kind things to us and about us, it warms our heart. It refreshes and revitalizes us. It is like they are on the sidelines of life, cheering us on. Their encouragement lifts us up and pushes us forward.

Encouragement is wonderful, but spiritual encouragement is life-giving. It speaks to a person's soul. It creates a place of safety. It shows the other person that they are important and that they are filled with beauty because

---

3. Hunt, Susan and Anyabwile, Kristie. 'Older and Younger: Taking Titus Seriously' *Word-Filled Women's Ministry: Loving and Serving the Church*, Eds. Gloria Furman and Kathleen B. Nielson (Wheaton, IL: Crossway, 2015), p. 167.

they are created in God's image. It sees Christ in the other person. It points out and acknowledges the work God is doing in another. It rejoices with others. Encouragement desires good for another and in all things points them to Christ.

Equipping involves teaching God's word to another. It involves helping them see how the gospel applies to every area of life. It involves preparing another for how to face trials that will certainly come. It involves Bible study and reading a Christ-centered book together. In terms of Titus 2 discipleship, it involves teaching 'what is good, and so train the young women to love their husbands and children, to be self-controlled, pure, working at home, kind, and submissive to their own husbands, that the word of God may not be reviled' (Titus 2:4-5).

It also involves prayer. As I shared at the beginning of the chapter, my spiritual mentor prayed with me at the hospital. Her words not only encouraged me, but they also equipped me. Her prayer reminded me that God was sovereign over all things. Her words also reminded me that God is faithful, good, and trustworthy.

There is much we learn from one another through prayer. Prayer itself can be a form of discipleship. As Megan Hill wrote in *Praying Together*, 'In praying together we disciple one another: we strengthen one another's faith, testifying to our experiences of God, shape one another's repentance and desires, stir one another to thanksgiving, and encourage one another in godly habits. In these things, too, we also help one another to resist various temptations to sin…At its heart, prayer is an invisible act of faith in an unseen God, and praying with others strengthens our own faith and silences our nagging doubts.'[4] Sisters, we need older women who pray for us and in hearing their prayers, we are trained, equipped, strengthened, encouraged, and shaped in the faith.

Such an encouraging/equipping relationship reminds us of the one Paul had with Timothy. 'To Timothy, my true child in the faith: Grace, mercy, and peace from God the Father and Christ Jesus our Lord' (1 Tim. 1:2). Paul encouraged and equipped Timothy in the faith, mentoring him in his role as pastor. His letters to Timothy are filled with instruction and encouragement to press forward in his call as shepherd. 'Fight the good fight of the faith. Take hold of the eternal life to which you were called and about which you made the good confession in the presence of many witnesses' (1 Tim. 6:12).

What does this all mean for us as we seek to have relationships with women in the church that are 'closer than a sister?' While discipleship between women is described as spiritual mothering, we are still sisters in the Lord. It's just that some of us are older in the faith than others. Among our relationships with sisters in the church, we need to have friendships with older women. We also need relationships with younger women. We need to be encouraged and equipped through Titus 2 discipleship as well as encourage and equip younger sisters in the faith.

In some churches, there are formal discipleship programs that have been established for older women to

---

4. Hill, Megan. *Praying Together: The Priority and Privilege of Prayer in Our Homes, Communities, and Churches* (Wheaton, IL: Crossway, 2016), pp. 70-71.

disciple younger women. If your church has one, consider joining one. Not every church has one but that's no reason not to be in a discipleship relationship. Pray and ask God to bring someone in your life that can disciple you. Pray for a younger woman whom you can encourage and equip in the faith.

Consider the older women in your church. Who radiates Christ? Who has inner beauty that overflows into how she loves others? Who is wise in the faith? Reach out to her and get to know her. Ask her questions about her faith and about God's work in her life. Ask to meet for prayer. Ask her if she would read a book with you and meet to talk about it.

You might be amazed at how many older women have been waiting for a younger woman to reach out to them for discipleship. A couple of years ago, my church's women's ministry team and I worked together to develop a Titus 2 discipleship program at our church. When I spoke with the women of the church about the program and went through the Titus 2 passage with them, I was amazed at how many older women were encouraged by the talk. It was as though they had been waiting in the wings to be invited out on stage. They were excited about the possibility of being used in such a way in the church. The whole process created new relationships for me with women I didn't know very well as older women came to me one by one to talk about discipleship and their desire to mentor other women.

Sisters learn together through discipleship. Consider how God might teach you through an older woman in your church.

Questions to Consider:

Read the Titus 2 mandate again. Have you ever had such a relationship with an older woman in the faith? How did she encourage and equip you?

Are there younger women in your life whom you can disciple?

These days, we get much of our information online. How would a flesh and blood discipleship relationship differ from what we can learn from reading blogs or engaging in online forums/discussions?

THOUGH
WE ARE ALL
INDIVIDUALS,
WE UNITE
TOGETHER TO
USE OUR GIFTS
FOR THE GOOD
OF THE CHURCH
AND THE GLORY
OF GOD.

9

Sisters Grow Together

'...we are to grow up in every way into him who is the head, into Christ.'
Ephesians 4:15

HAVE you ever been house hunting? I enjoy watching shows on television where couples look at houses to buy. It's interesting the choices they make and why they do so. I prefer neighborhoods where each house is different in some way. I don't like 'cookie cutter' houses where each house is the exact replica of the one beside it. In fact, since moving into our new neighborhood, my husband and I enjoy going for walks together and looking at the different houses in the neighborhood. We like the diversity in style, size, color, and layout.

I think that God likes diversity too. After all, look at the creation around you. The varying shapes, colors, and patterns of the natural world are widely diverse. The sheer number of different beetles that exist on planet earth is astounding. Each person we meet is unique from the next, right down to the swirls on each of their fingertips.

Then there is the diversity we find in the church. The Bride of Christ is made up of saints from all nations, of every skin color, and of each language, 'After this I looked, and behold, a great multitude that no one could number, from every nation, from all tribes and peoples and languages, standing before the throne and before the Lamb, clothed in white robes, with palm branches in their hands' (Rev. 7:9). This beautiful assembly will one day unite together as one to glorify and sing praises to the One who created all things.

Diversity of Gifts, Unity in Gifts

One area in the church where we see variety is in the way God has gifted the saints. The *Westminster Confession* uses the words 'gifts and graces' to describe the virtues and abilities which God gives us as Christians. 'All saints, that are united to Jesus Christ their Head...being united to one another in love, they have communion in each other's gifts and graces, and are obliged to the performance of such duties...'[1] Graces are more like attributes and characteristics such as love, kindness, humility, and forbearance (see also Gal. 5:22). They are used alongside our gifts and enable us to use our gifts for the benefit of the church. Gifts are those God-given abilities we have to serve the church, such as teaching, showing mercy, and extending hospitality.

---

1. Williamson, G.I. *The Westminster Confession of Faith: For Study Classes* (Philipsburg, NJ: P&R Publishing, 1964), p. 196.

We do not all have the same gifts and graces. We are not all teachers or preachers or administrators. We do not all have the same levels of patience, compassion, or gratitude, nor do we have them all at the same time. Though we all have different gifts, they all come from the same God who uses them for His Kingdom purposes. 'Now there are varieties of gifts, but the same Spirit; and there are varieties of service, but the same Lord; and there are varieties of activities, but it is the same God who empowers them all in everyone' (1 Cor. 12:4-6).

The main metaphor that Paul used to describe the church and how each of our differing gifts work together is that of a human body. The human body is made up of many parts (206 bones alone!). Each part works together to make the body function and keep it alive. Some parts of the human body are more prominent while others are hidden. Some are merely ordinary. But each part is necessary. So too, the church is made up of many people with many different gifts. Each part is important and essential to the life of the church.

1 Corinthians 12:12-27:

For just as the body is one and has many members, and all the members of the body, though many, are one body, so it is with Christ. For in one Spirit we were all baptized into one body – Jews or Greeks, slaves or free – and all were made to drink of one Spirit. For the body does not consist of one member but of many. If the foot should say, 'Because I am not a hand, I do not belong to the body,' that would not make it any less a part of the body. And if the ear should say, 'Because I am not an eye, I do not belong to the body,' that would not make it any less a part of the body. If the whole body were an eye, where would be the sense of hearing? If the whole body were an ear, where would be the sense of smell? But as it is, God arranged the members in the body, each one of them, as he chose. If all were a single member, where would the body be? As it is, there are many parts, yet one body. The eye cannot say to the hand, 'I have no need of you,' nor again the head to the feet, 'I have no need of you.' On the contrary, the parts of the body that seem to be weaker are indispensable, and on those parts of the body that we think less honorable we bestow the greater honor, and our unpresentable parts are treated with greater modesty, which our more presentable parts do not require. But God has so composed the body, giving greater honor to the part that lacked it, that there may be no division in the body, but that the members may have the same care for one another. If one member suffers, all suffer together; if one member is honored, all rejoice together. Now you are the body of Christ and individually members of it.

Though there is diversity in the church, there is also unity. Though we are all individuals, we are also part of a united whole. We unite together to use our gifts for the good of the church and the glory of God. 'Christ gives spiritual gifts and graces to adorn and equip the church for the work it is called to do…The purpose of God's giving gifts and graces is communal, not personal. My spiritual gifts are not my own; they belong to Christ and to his church.'[2]

It is God who designed the Body and gave us our gifts according to His pleasure and will, 'All these are empowered by one and the same Spirit, who apportions to each one

2. Ryken, p. 100.

individually as he wills' (1 Cor. 12:11). This means there is no place for comparison, envy, looking down on others, or feeling inferior because our gifts are different than others. Though some members have gifts that are highlighted more than others, it doesn't make them more important. We can't treat those who are teachers or worship leaders as more essential to the church than those who rock babies in the nursery or who bring meals to the elderly. Just like the human body, each member of the church Body is essential and important and as we work together, we keep the church functioning and healthy.

As Paul wrote in Romans 12:3-8:

> For by the grace given to me I say to everyone among you not to think of himself more highly than he ought to think, but to think with sober judgment, each according to the measure of faith that God has assigned. For as in one body we have many members, and the members do not all have the same function, so we, though many, are one body in Christ, and individually members one of another. Having gifts that differ according to the grace given to us, let us use them: if prophecy, in proportion to our faith; if service, in our serving; the one who teaches, in his teaching; the one who exhorts, in his exhortation; the one who contributes, in generosity; the one who leads, with zeal; the one who does acts of mercy, with cheerfulness.

We also ought to celebrate and rejoice over our diversity of gifts and graces. As Lane and Tripp wrote, 'Because it is grounded in the Trinity, our unity also allows us to celebrate our diversity in the body of Christ. There is one God, but three persons. God uses our diversity to accomplish his purpose – our growth in grace. Diversity is not an obstacle, but a very significant means to an end.'[3]

In our Reformed tradition, and in keeping with God's word, men alone are called by God to serve the church as pastors and elders (see Titus 1 and 1 Tim. 3). However, God has not left women without gifts to use in service to the church. Women have the gift of teaching, serving, encouraging, mercy, administration, and more. We might teach Bible studies, Sunday school, and discipleship groups. We might serve behind the scenes by providing meals to the hungry or setting up for our monthly church supper. We might meet with other young moms and encourage them with the gospel. We might sing Bible songs with preschoolers or write notes to the homebound. We might serve on the mission team or prepare bulletins for Sunday worship. We might play the piano for Sunday worship or meet with teen girls for prayer and Bible study. Whatever our gifts, we are to use them and to do so with cheerfulness, not despising our gifts or begrudging the gifts others have.

As the *Heidelberg Catechism* asks:

Q: What do you understand by the communion of saints?

A: First, that believers, all and everyone, as members of Christ have communion with him and share in all his treasures and gifts. Second, that everyone is duty-bound to use his gifts readily and cheerfully for the benefit and well-being of the other members.

---

3. Lane and Tripp, p. 47.

Sisters Grow Together

At my previous church, we had been without an official women's ministry for nearly ten years. God answered our prayers and I was able to work together with a team of other women in the church, with the support and oversight of the session, to develop a women's ministry. One of my goals for the women's ministry was to draw in and utilize the varying gifts of the women in the congregation.

In every church there are people who stand out in ministry. We all know who they are. They always step up to serve and their gifts are ones that are most prevalent and noticeable to us: they sing on the worship team, they lead the children's ministry, or they teach a women's Bible study. There are also many other women in the church who also have gifts. Perhaps their gifts are used more in the background and behind the scenes, but they are important nonetheless. Or perhaps because they aren't gifted to serve in prominent roles, they might think they are not useful to the church. These are women who need encouragement to see that they are just as important to the Body as others.

As we developed our women's ministry, we sought out these women and found places for them to serve in our women's ministry. We developed teams where women could use their gifts of administration, mercy, and service, as well as those of teaching and discipleship. We utilized those who were prayer warriors to join with other prayer warriors to pray for the church. We found those who had the gift of mercy and encouraged them to work together with others who also had the gift of mercy to consider ways they could serve the church and the community. Those who were creative and artistic worked together to make things beautiful for the church. We developed each team to have a combination of older and younger women, working side by side, for the glory of Christ and His church.[4]

Watching my sisters in the Lord work together in this way was beautiful. I saw people who had previously been on the sidelines realize that they were needed, that they had a purpose, and that they were important. I saw older and younger women learn from one another, encourage one another, and grow closer to one another. I saw people eager to serve and grow the church for the glory of God.

Sisters, when we work together in our local churches, we grow together. When we serve together with a united heart to see the Kingdom spread, we grow together. We also grow together when we encourage and honor one another in using the gifts God gives us. And when we are united, using our gifts side-by-side, we grow together and build up the church in love. 'We are to grow up in every way into him who is the head, into Christ, from whom the whole body, joined and held together by every joint with which it is equipped, when each part is working properly, makes the body grow so that it builds itself up in love' (Eph. 4:15-16).

---

4. I am grateful to my sister-friends and mentors, Karen Hodge, Martha Hansen, and Linda Watts for their help and guidance in helping me strategize and develop the women's ministry team. Their wisdom and experience was a blessing and I couldn't have done it without them. Another example of how God uses older women to disciple younger women!

Certainly, every church has its own polity and manner in which it utilizes each member's gifts. The example I gave of how our women's ministry used our gifts was just that, an example to show the beauty of our diversity working together in unity. The method isn't what's important. What is important is that we all use our gifts for the good of the church so that it grows and builds itself up in love.

Remain in Christ

As we consider our gifts and how to use them to serve the church, we have to remember our unity with Christ. The fruit we produce as believers comes only from our connection to the Vine of Christ. 'I am the vine; you are the branches. Whoever abides in me and I in him, he it is that bears much fruit, for apart from me you can do nothing' (John 15:5). We can't produce any gifts or graces on our own; it is Christ's work through us that produces fruit. We can't love one another apart from Christ. We can't show patience or give forgiveness apart from Christ. We can't teach, serve, or encourage apart from Christ. Christ is our source and sustenance for all the work we do.

When we start to think that we have no use in the church, we need to ask ourselves whether we are abiding in the Vine or trying to live on our own. If we find ourselves wishing we had different gifts or comparing our gifts to others or even begrudging our sister's gifts, we need to evaluate our heart and repent. When we think that there is no purpose or reason to be part of a church, we have forgotten our unity with Christ and others in the faith. 'A Christian cut off from the fellowship of the saints and separated from the fellowship of the whole body of Christ will become stunted and virtually lifeless.'[5]

Our Father is a good and faithful Father. He is generous to us and gives us all that we need. Therefore, we need to seek Him and pray that He would provide us with gifts and graces. If we don't know what our gifts are, we need to learn what they are. We need to be thankful for the gifts we are given and use them gratefully and cheerfully. We also need to remember that they are not for our benefit but for the good and growth of the church.

Questions to Consider:

Read Ephesians 4:1-16. How many 'ones' does Paul mention in verses 4-6? This unity is the theological foundation for how we serve and work together in the Body.

Learn more about the spiritual gifts God gives us: Romans 12:6-8 and 1 Corinthians 12.

Have you ever taken a spiritual gifts inventory? If not, ask your church leadership to help you take one.

Have you ever seen the diversity of gifts among the women in your church used together in unity?

---

5. Ryken, p. 101.

PART III

*Challenges
in Sisterhood*

GOD
CREATES
COMMUNITY,
BUT WE
HAVE TO
CULTIVATE
AND
NURTURE IT.

10

Cultivating Community

'You can't stay in your corner of the Forest waiting for others to come to you. You have to go to them sometimes.'

A. A. MILNE [1]

SO far in this book, I've attempted to paint a picture of Christian friendship, specifically friendship among women in the church. We've looked at the theological reasons for our friendships with others in the church. We've looked at our union with Christ and with one another. We've also looked at specific descriptions of what these friendships look like. We've looked at practical ways we can love and serve one another. We've discovered that relationships with others

---

1. Milne, A. A. (edited by Shepard, Ernest H.), *Pooh's Little Instruction Book* (New York: Dutton, 1995).

in the family of God are real and honest and that God uses us in the Body to help one another grow in the faith.

As you read along, you might have thought to yourself, 'Ok, I understand the theology behind our relationships. I see the picture you've painted of sisterhood. But that's not the reality in my church. Women in my church are not that connected with one another.' Or perhaps you thought, 'I've tried that before. I opened up to the women in my Bible study and they looked at me like I was from outer space. I was humiliated.' Or 'I've had close friendships like that before and ended up hurt and rejected. It's just not worth it.'

Community and friendship in the church *is* hard. It is not easy. We are all broken and sinful and one of the places we see that most is in our interactions with others. Finding friendships like the ones I described in this book is challenging and it's even more challenging to keep them. I say that because I spent many years seeking such friendships and have lost many friendships along the way. But despite the heartache and the challenges, I believe it *is* worth it.

Jesus thought so. He went to great lengths to redeem the church, His Bride. Though she was fickle, wayward, and adulterous, He bought her with His own blood. Since our Savior believes the church is worth it, we should too.

Cultivating Community

Over twenty years ago now, I attended Covenant College, a Christian liberal arts college. The culture of the college was community centered. It was a small college so we all knew each other, or at least recognized each other as fellow students. The class sizes were small so we knew the professors well, sometimes even meeting for class in their homes. The RAs on each hall in the dormitory often led hall devotions. We shared with our hallmates and roommates whatever we had, just like a family would do. We even had a day of prayer each semester where classes were cancelled and we gathered together as a community to pray.

In this environment, I learned and grew in my understanding of community and of our connectedness to one another as believers. I participated in my first accountability/prayer group there with two other girls. Many of the friends I made in college are still my closest friends today.

After I left college and got married, my husband and I moved away from that tight-knit community. As we settled into our new town, new home, and new jobs, we also found a new church and expected to find the same kind of community we had in college. We didn't. Sure, everyone was warm and kind and friendly. But it was hard to engage people at the level of honesty we were used to. At first we were discouraged. I missed my friends and my community. I despaired of ever finding a community where I could truly know others and also be known by my community. Slowly, my husband and I came to realize that while our college had a ready-made community available for us, now that we were on our own, we would have to work to cultivate it ourselves.

God creates community but we have to cultivate and nurture it. Even though a church meets together every Sunday, that doesn't mean the church members automatically live out the community I've described in this book. It takes hard work and intention to nurture that community. The seeds are there but we have to water them to help them grow.

Perhaps that is why finding community and friendships through social media is so appealing these days. It takes less work and effort. I've found myself at times thinking about the friends I have met through online networks, 'I wish they lived near me, I bet we'd be the best of friends' or 'Why aren't any of my local friends as encouraging as she is?' But then I have to remind myself that the few minutes I spend engaging with someone online is far different than living in community with that person.

In community, we rub up against each other. We see each other's facial expressions when we share about our life. We know right away whether they agree with us or even understand us. We see their imperfections and weaknesses first hand, and they see ours. We experience disappointment when they don't reciprocate our hospitality or are chronically late for play dates with our kids. We see the depths of their struggles in ways we'd never see from an online friend and they see the same in us.

Real life friendships are harder than online relationships. They take more work and effort. Exchanging a few texts, emails, or messages with a friend in another state or country requires minimal involvement. Sharing real flesh and blood life with the sisters in our local churches is messier and makes us more vulnerable to hurt and disappointment. But at the same time, an online friend would never stop by our house and bring us a meal when we're sick. An online friend wouldn't know us well enough to know the gospel truth our heart needs to hear at just the right moment. An online friend cannot sit with us at the hospital while we await news of a loved one. An online friend can't hug us during Sunday worship when they see the tears streaming down our face.

Despite the hard work involved, real sister-friendships are worth it. After all, that is how God responded to our greatest need. He didn't address the problem of sin from far away; He engaged it face to face. He took on flesh and blood and lived among us, becoming sin for us so that we could have His righteousness. When it comes to engaging with the messy lives of our sisters, and they with us, how can we do no less than what our Savior did for us?

How do we cultivate real, honest, relationships with other women in our church? How can we develop and sustain them?

Pray for Deeper Friendships

If you are at a church where you desire to see rich friendships develop and grow, seek God in prayer. God is the creator of community. It is His idea that we be united and connected to one another. Praying for something that He desires is a prayer He loves to answer. Pray for God to give you wisdom in how to reach out to others in your church. Pray for opportunities to grow in deeper friendships with others. Pray that God would bring you the friendships you need most. Pray for relationships with older and younger women. Pray for trustworthy friendships and for discernment to know when a friendship is not safe for you. Pray that you would be a good friend to someone else.

Participate in Your Church Body

'They devoted themselves to the apostles' teaching and to fellowship, to the breaking of bread and to prayer...

Every day they continued to meet together in the temple courts. They broke bread in their homes and ate together with glad and sincere hearts' (Acts 2:42, 46). The early church met together not only for worship, but as often as they could. They worshipped, learned, prayed, and fellow-shipped together. These days, churches are trimming back the times they spend together. Fewer churches offer Sunday school or Sunday evening worship. Wednesday night prayer meeting seems like a relic of the past. In our fast-paced, busy life we make little margin for meeting with our church family.

Yet the best way to get to know other people in the church is to participate in whatever activities, studies, worship times, and other gatherings your church offers. You'll never connect with others if you always arrive to church late and are the first one to leave. When it comes to the women of the church, one of the best ways to get to know other women is through the women's ministry. Most women's ministries have a weekly Bible study. Attend the study and be intentional about meeting the women there and getting to know them. If your women's ministry has an annual retreat or goes out of town for an event or conference, go with them. Retreats and conferences are excellent ways to get to know other people. When we spend uninterrupted time traveling with others, eating meals together, and learning together, we often forge deep, lasting friendships.

Many churches also have some kind of small group Bible study that meets in people's homes. This is another excellent way to get to know other women. Sitting in some-one's living room and talking about God's word opens the door to intimate conversations about what God is doing in each other's lives. You can't help but get to know people when you are in a small group setting.

Participate in the fellowship time your church offers, whether it is coffee time before the service or the monthly fellowship dinner in the church gym. Go up to people and ask them about their week. Find out what they do with their time. Learn about their hobbies and interests. These simple social interactions provide the opportunity to discover shared interests and experiences.

Most relationships start with introductions and learning basic facts about one another. As you participate in church activities, be intentional to meet others and learn about them. In our previous church, another family and ours would often challenge each other to meet someone new each Sunday and then we'd follow up with each other and ask who we met and what we learned about them. This challenge kept us from only talking to the people with whom we already felt comfortable.

As you meet people, ask open-ended questions (ones they can't answer with a yes or no response) and show them that you really care to know them. Over time you'll find people who have similar interests, similar experiences, and similar hopes and dreams. Continue developing these relationships. Meet for coffee outside of church or invite them over to your house for a meal. Relationships take time to grow but they also take regular contact and engagement. You can't expect a relationship to grow and thrive just by seeing each other only on Sunday mornings. Deep friendships require more than that.

In *How Should We Develop Biblical Friendship?*, authors Beeke and Haykin point out that a good way to look at our friendships is through that of levels of closeness – as concentric circles of mutual trust and knowledge.[2] Think of a target, the kind at which you throw darts or shoot arrows. Those closest to us are those we trust the most and those who know the most about us. They would be in the circle at the very center of the target. Then there are those whom we might consider friends because we spend much time with them in our work or serve alongside them in ministry but they don't know everything about us. These friends would be in the ring around the center of the circle. Then there are those on the next ring, with whom we might share common goals but we wouldn't consider them good friends. And then on the furthest ring away from the center are those who are more like acquaintances, people whom we might have met and know a few facts about but with whom we have little connection.

Most of our relationships in church will begin in the outer rings of the circle, as acquaintances. Through time spent together in service or in attending Bible studies together we might get to know them more. Some of these people will move inward on the circle as we learn more about them and as we grow in our mutual trust of one another. Until finally, there are those sister-friends, with whom through time and patience, the fruit of deep friendship is born.

To be sure, not everyone in our church will be in that inner circle of deep trust and knowledge. That would be impossible. Some of the characteristics of friendships we have discussed in this book will be true of most of our

---

2. Beeke, Joel R. and Haykin, Michael A. *How Should We Develop Biblical Friendship?* (Grand Rapids, MI: Reformation Heritage Books, 2015), p. 23.

friendships in the church (such as helping one another and serving together) and others will only be true of those in our inner circle (such as those who hold us accountable).

Open Your Door in Hospitality

Hospitality is the main way my husband and I learned to cultivate relationships. After we recovered from the initial shock of being in a new community and having to start over in making friends, we decided to invite people from our church over to our house. Because we knew what it felt like to be new to a church, we made it a habit to meet new families who came to visit our church and invited them to share a meal with us.

Inviting someone to your home is a good first step to opening your heart to someone else. But I have to admit, hospitality does not come naturally to me. I often get wrapped up in the details of hospitality. I worry about making food that people don't like or that there won't be enough seating or that my house isn't clean enough. I exhaust myself in preparing for guests that I'm often too tired to participate in the reason why I've invited guests over to begin with. Slowly but surely, the Lord has worked on my heart in these areas and shown me that the details are not as important as engaging the hearts of my guests. I've learned over the years that when I welcome people into my home, I mirror the love of Christ who through His sacrifice has made a way for me to enter His home and be with Him forever.

As we gather around a table layered with food to meet our physical hunger, we join with other children of the Father, all in need of spiritual food to satisfy our hungry souls. When we share a meal with our brothers and sisters in the Lord, we share our mutual love of the Bread of Life. When we are refreshed with drink, we can share in our mutual need for the Living Water, the only water that satisfies. It is a splendid thing to enjoy food and drink with our sisters and brothers, to give thanks together and feast on the blessings God has given. And even more so, to share in the spiritual food that is our Savior.

Yet hospitality doesn't always mean inviting someone over for dinner. When my kids were young, I often hosted play groups at my house. There were times when there were upwards of ten babies crawling all around my living room. These were great times of fellowship as we encouraged one another in our mothering. It was a way of living life together, sharing in the challenges and sanctifying growth of motherhood.

My husband and I have also hosted small group Bible studies, discipleship groups, church fellowship events, holiday parties, and more in our home. These times produced sweet and lasting memories with people in our church where we were able to connect and talk in a relaxing atmosphere. Some of these events became yearly traditions that we all looked forward to.

Hospitality looks different for each person but I encourage anyone who desires to develop deeper friendships to open their door in hospitality. It's an invitation, not to a structure, but into your very life. When guests come into my house, they see the Nerf-dart littered floors, the unopened mail on the counter, and the dirty football cleats by the stairs. They see the real stuff of life in my home – the chaos and unpredictability, the sibling spats and my impatient responses, the piles of things yet to put away.

Among all the noise is a place to be real and share about the challenges and hardships of life. Hospitality provides an opportunity and place to be known and mutually encouraged. Hospitality makes a way for community.

Serve Your Sisters

Another way to cultivate relationships is through service. When we reach out to someone who needs help in our church, we can't help but get to know them. One easy way to serve someone is by bringing a meal to their home. Whether it is a homebound widow, someone recovering from surgery, or a new mom, a homemade meal is something everyone appreciates and it helps facilitate relationships. I once brought a meal to a new mom from our church that I didn't know. I ended up sitting down at her kitchen table and answered her questions about motherhood and parenting. I then went back the following week and played with her toddler while she rested with her new baby. And I made a new friend in the process.

Another way to serve someone is to help a family move. When we moved to our house from another state, people at our new church came over to help us. These were people we didn't know and who didn't know us, but we got to know them because they came and served us.

There are always people in the church who could use an extra hand in some way. Consider the older women in your church, especially the widows. Think of ways you could love and serve them. Perhaps they need help with minor house repair or yard work. Not only are there countless ways you could serve them, but there is much you could learn from them as well.

Lastly, another practical way to serve someone is when you hear that someone in your church is hurting, reach out to them. Send them a note in the mail. Stop by their house and bring them a loaf of bread or plate of cookies. Tell them you are praying for them. Better yet, take the time to sit with them and pray for them.

Take the First Step and Model Community

The characteristics we explored in this book are ones that often many people don't naturally know how to do. It doesn't come naturally to us to share our burdens or voice our struggles or talk about our doubts, sorrows, and temptations. Sometimes we have to be the one who initiates and takes that first step. As we open up about our own struggles, we model for others what Christian sisterhood looks like.

In a small group Bible study one morning, I shared with the women there that I have a history of depression. I voiced concern that I felt myself struggling with depressive thoughts and wanted prayer about it. Such a prayer request was different than the normal prayer requests for health and healing, for houses to sell, or a job to be found. Yet it was a pressing need for me so I decided to voice it. Another woman in the group came up to me after the study and talked with me about it. She was kind and encouraging and it opened up the opportunity for our relationship to go deeper.

As I wrote in an earlier chapter, we don't need to go up to complete strangers in the church and bare our soul. But those relationships we have developed through participating in church each Sunday and in other church activities are the friendships we can take steps to deepen. We can take the initiative and ask them to pray for a specific struggle. 'Could you pray for me? I am struggling with trusting God right now since my husband has been out of work.' Or 'Would you like to meet for prayer and coffee one day this week?' We could also ask them, 'How can I pray for you this coming week?'

We are all used to talking with one another about sports, the weather, our children, and our jobs that we often need a push to take conversations to a deeper level. Such conversations will not happen unless one person takes the risk and starts it. It might feel uncomfortable. Doing anything out of the ordinary feels awkward at first. But it is worth it when doing so cultivates friendship that encourages us and spurs us forward in our faith.

Ultimately, to cultivate friendship, we have to *be* a friend. We often look for others who will be a friend to us, but the place to start is to *be* a friend to others. Be the friend you desire to have.

When People Don't Desire Community

Here's where I have to get honest. I have had relationships where I have opened up about the struggles, challenges, and battles against sin in my life but the other person did not reciprocate. The silence was heavy; I could almost hear the sound of crickets. This is challenging and frustrating and often makes us not want to take that risk again, but we can't let that stop us. Some people are just not ready for the kind of friendship we desire. Not everyone is, at least not yet. Perhaps they are new to the faith and there is more for them to learn first. Perhaps they have their own wounds from broken friendships in the past that keep them from trusting others. Sometimes there are even cultural obstacles to this type of friendship. Whatever the reason, though it might be frustrating, disappointing, or disconcerting, we can't think unkindly of them but rather, need to have forbearance for them. 'Put on then, as God's chosen ones, holy and beloved, compassionate hearts, kindness, humility, meekness, and patience' (Col. 3:12).

It took many years of me reaching out to people in my church community and initiating honest friendships with them before the Lord brought several women into my life who desired the same level of friendship that I did. And to be honest, by that time, I was disappointed and almost cynical of Christian friendship but the Lord used these new friends to bring healing. They showed me that in fact there *are* people who will sit in the dust and ashes and mourn with one another. They showed me that there *are* friends who will stick closer than a sister, who want to learn together, grow together, serve together, and spur one another on to love and good deeds. These friendships *do* exist and are worth the wait and the time invested.

When the idea for this book first sparked to life, I was on vacation with this same group of dear friends. Several families from church would gather together each summer and rent a house together for a week. It was a rich time of fellowship, encouragement, rest, and fun. As I enjoyed this time with my friends, I considered the idea of writing about community, our need for it, and what it looks like. At that time in my life, I was in a good place with my community. I had several close sister-friends and several others with whom I was growing in friendship. I approached my publisher about this topic and they decided to wait a year first.

By the time I submitted the topic again, I had lost my community. Dear friends moved away. Our church went through a significant change and many people left. Then we ended up moving away to another state.

When my publisher said yes to the idea for a book about Christian friendship among women in the church, I thought, 'How can I write about community and friendship when I have lost mine?' And so it was that I wrote this book, in many ways, community-less. We were in a new church, in a new state. I had to re-learn and practice these very same lessons I've written about here. I had to cultivate community. I had to be vulnerable and take risks. I had to reach out and ask for help and prayer. I had to initiate and invite people into my life.

Even now, I am in the midst of cultivating community. I know it will be a long process. I know it will be hard. I know that some people will not be interested. I know there will be challenges along the way. But I believe in community. I believe in Christian friendship as the Bible describes. Our Savior believed the Bride was worth the effort, and I do too.

Questions to Consider:

Read I Peter I and then focus on I Peter I:22-23. How does the gospel impact how we live out the command to 'love one another earnestly from a pure heart'?

I Peter 4:9 says, 'Show hospitality to one another without grumbling.' Does this instruction challenge you? Why or why not? Who could you reach out to in hospitality today?

What kinds of disappointments have you experienced in friendship in the past? How have these disappointments shaped the way you view friendship today?

THOUGH
OUR
FRIENDS
MAY
FORSAKE
US, OUR
SAVIOR
NEVER
WILL.

11

Challenges to Community

'And the Lord turned and looked at Peter.
And Peter remembered the saying of the
Lord, how he had said to him, "Before the
rooster crows today, you will deny me three
times." And he went out and wept bitterly.'
LUKE 22:61-62

I remember the first time I lost a friend. I was nine years old and my best friend from school moved away. I still remember crying in my room the afternoon after I heard the news. It was devastating to my young heart. I didn't think I'd ever have another friend again.

Of course I have had many friends since that time. Many of those have been close, dear friends. But over time those relationships have changed. Some of those friends I haven't seen in twenty years. Some relationships simply faded over time. Other friendships ended for reasons I never learned or understood. And then there were those that ended in tears.

When a Friend Rejects Us

I'll probably never forget the words my friend said to me, words that cut deep into my heart. We had been good friends for many years and to hear her words of rejection left me staggering. If it were possible, my heart hurt. Everything I thought I knew about her and our friendship was left shattered and in pieces. My mind rehearsed all my memories of our relationship with suspicion. I scrolled back through the years of our friendship and wondered if I was wrong about everything I had believed about our friendship. And then, as a result, I started to withdraw from others to protect myself from further hurt and rejection. Worse than that, I harbored anger and bitterness in my heart.

Perhaps you've had a similar situation when a close friend rejected you and cut off your friendship. When we have invested in a relationship over a period of time and share memories and experiences with a dear friend and then they turn their backs on us in rejection, it is painful. David knew this pain and wrote about it in Psalm 55, 'For it is not an enemy who taunts me – then I could bear it; it is not an adversary who deals insolently with me – then I could hide from him. But it is you, a man, my equal, my companion, my familiar friend. We used to take sweet counsel together; within God's house we walked in the throng' (vv. 12-14).

The wounds of a friend hurt worse than those of an enemy. As David wrote, 'for it is not an enemy who taunts me – then I could bear it.' David's friend was someone with whom he went and worshipped the Lord. When our believing friends reject us, this is especially painful. When people with whom we are united together in the faith, people with whom we share the common bond of sisterhood – when sister-friends reject us, it seems unbearable.

In the face of rejection, we must remember our Savior. The sorrow we feel over broken relationships can remind us of the One who was broken for us. 'He was despised and rejected by men; a man of sorrows, and acquainted with grief' (Isa. 53:3).

Jesus was rejected by His dear friend Peter when He was on trial; three times Peter denied knowing Him. He was rejected by those He had grown up with in His hometown of Nazareth (Mark 6:4). When He was arrested, all His disciples fled and abandoned Him when He needed them most (Matt. 26:31). On the cross, Jesus bore the full weight of rejection for us when the Father poured out His wrath upon Him for our sins.

After He rose from the grave, Jesus came and found Peter. 'When they had finished breakfast, Jesus said to Simon Peter, "Simon, son of John, do you love me more than these?" He said to him, "Yes, Lord; you know that I love you." He said to him, "Feed my lambs."' (John 21:15). Jesus gently restored and brought Peter back into relationship with Himself. Though Peter had rejected Him, Jesus gave him grace.

Though our friends may forsake us, our Savior never will. His love for us is not dependent on anything we have done; it will not waver and will never change. We can trust Him and His love for us. He understands our sorrow and comforts us in it with His always faithful love.

When We Lose a Friend

One year our church went through a difficult season. There were conflicts between some of the church members and the leadership, details of which I knew nothing about, which resulted in several families leaving our church. Then a few more left. Then a few more. Each time a family left, I felt the loss as though it were a death. These people were my friends, my family in the Lord. Many of the women I had served in women's ministry with. Others had been with me in a weekly play group with our kids. Even though they all still lived in the same town, I knew things would never be the same. And they weren't. The connection and bond we had from being a part of the same church was broken. In truth, it felt like a divorce.

A couple of years ago, one of my dearest friends moved far away to another state. It was heartbreaking. We did everything together. Our kids participated in the same sports and activities. We traveled together as families. We took turns having meals together when our husbands were out of town for work. My everyday life changed drastically after her move. The months following were a difficult season of learning to trust in God's good plan.

For five years, I met with the same group of moms several times a week for playdates with our young children. We took turns hosting play times in our homes. We met at local parks. Our children all took music class together. We were all a part of each other's weekly routine. Then our kids all started school and everything changed. We got involved in other things and gradually drifted apart. We were still all friends, but we had all entered a different season of life and things changed.

No doubt about it, losing a friend is hard, especially a sister-friend in the Lord. Whatever the reason for the loss, whether it is a life change or a move or some other circumstance, it hurts. Like all losses, it takes time to grieve. Learning to go about our routine without our friend or friends is an adjustment.

A loss or change to a relationship is a challenge to community. Sometimes these losses can make it hard for us to develop new friendships. Sometimes we want to pull back and protect ourselves from further hurt. Sometimes we feel like we've lost our identity and our place. In those times, it is tempting to distance ourselves from others. As hard as it is, we need to continue to participate in our church community. We need to continue to pour into others. We need to serve and use our gifts. As we do so, we need to pray that the Lord would heal our hurts and comfort us. For He knows and cares about all our sorrows, 'You have kept count of my tossings; put my tears in your bottle. Are they not in your book?' (Ps. 56:8).

Even while we mourn the loss of a friendship, we can rejoice knowing that all our friends in the Lord are forever friends. Our parting is only temporary. One day, we will live and worship together once again, this time before the throne of God. 'No longer will there be anything accursed, but the throne of God and of the Lamb will be in it, and his servants will worship him. They will see his face, and his name will be on their foreheads. And night will be no more. They will need no light of lamp or sun, for the Lord

God will be their light, and they will reign forever and ever' (Rev. 22:3-5).

Social Media and Loneliness

In the introduction to this book, I asked the question, 'How many friends do you have?' Perhaps you tallied up your Facebook friends, Twitter and Instagram followers, connections on LinkedIn, and all the other social media connections you have. When you consider the number of people you are connected with, do you feel loved and cared for?

Social scientists have pointed out that though we are connected to hundreds of people through social media, we are lonelier than ever before. It seems ironic, doesn't it? 'Yet within this world of instant and absolute communication, unbounded by limits of time or space, we suffer from unprecedented alienation. We have never been more detached from one another, or lonelier. In a world consumed by ever more novel modes of socializing, we have less and less actual society. We live in an accelerating contradiction: the more connected we become, the lonelier we are. We were promised a global village; instead we inhabit the drab cul-de-sacs and endless freeways of a vast suburb of information.'[1]

Researchers disagree over whether social media is the cause of loneliness or whether lonely people are more likely to use social media. One researcher who studied the impact of social media on loneliness found that the more face to face social interactions people had, the less lonely they were.[2]

---

1. Marche, Stephen. 'Is Facebook Making Us Lonely?', *The Atlantic*, March 2012 www.theatlantic.com/magazine/archive/2012/05/is-facebook-making-us-lonely/308930/. Accessed 10/21/16.

2. Marche, Stephen.

He didn't blame loneliness on social media and instead said that it depends on how people use it. If we use social media to increase our face to face contact with one another, it becomes a good thing. But if we use it to avoid flesh and blood interaction, it contributes to our loneliness.

Researchers at Oregon Health and Science University did a study with older adults to learn what kind of social interactions or lack thereof might predict a person being diagnosed with depression. What they learned was that only face-to-face contact made any difference; virtual connections made no impact.[3]

The truth is, engaging with people face to face and living life together is a fading reality in our society today. In the past, community was already made for us and we just slipped right in and became a part of it. But today things are different. More people work at home and in isolation from others. We engage with our friends through an intermediary: a phone, device, or a computer. We don't know how to relate to people like we once did. We live life at top speed and think that a quick text is a realistic substitute for face to face interaction.

In this way, social media can be a challenge to Christian community. So much of our time is spent scrolling through our feeds that we think we don't have time to meet a friend for coffee. When we do talk to a friend at church, there's not much to say because we've already seen everything they did during the week on Instagram. Or because we've exchanged messages with a friend on social media, we think we have

3. Pinker, Susan. 'To Beat the Blues, Visit Must Be Real, Not Virtual', *The Washington Post* June 2, 2016 www.wsj.com/articles/to-beat-the-blues-visits-must-be-real-not-virtual-1464899707. Accessed 10/21/16.

connected with them when in fact we haven't because such connection is only an illusion. Friendships that exist only on social media or through a mediated device are only a mirage of real friendship. They look like friendship but don't have any of the expectations, requirements, and demands that real, face to face, friendships call for.

Social media is fun and entertaining. It connects us to people we might not have seen in years. I love seeing pictures of my niece on Instagram or scrolling through my feed on Facebook and clicking on the latest article from my favorite author. I enjoy sharing with others the exciting events and even mundane happenings in my life. But social media can never be a substitute for real, flesh and blood community. Though we might feel connected with people online because we know what they are doing in their daily lives (and sometimes, minute by minute!), it's not the same thing as being with them in person. There is nothing wrong with liking our friend's photos or sending quick messages to friends far away, but we must remember that it can't take the place of face to face community. And we can't let it interfere with real connections with real people in real life.

Circular Loneliness

Some of us experience loneliness of a different kind in our churches: circular loneliness. Have you ever been in church, surrounded by people talking about their week, yet you felt utterly alone? Perhaps you are new to the church and don't know many people. Perhaps you have been busy with work or school or have been out of town and have been in worship intermittently. You feel disconnected from the Body. You might think to yourself, 'I don't know anyone and no one knows me. I don't belong here.' This makes you feel even more alone and disconnected. Because you don't feel like you belong, you attend church less often. You stop going to church events and gatherings. And as a result you feel even more disconnected until finally, you stop attending there altogether.

I call this circular loneliness. We feel lonely for some reason and our loneliness makes us less likely to interact with others, which only increases our loneliness. We feel disconnected so we disconnect from our church. It's circular and keeps going round and round.

The only way a circle stops being a circle is when it is cut. When we walk into church feeling lonely, we have to initiate and reach out to people. Instead of waiting for someone to talk to us, we have to talk to others. This goes against how we are feeling. When we feel lonely, our tendency is to want to withdraw more but we have to do the opposite. We have to engage with people, invite them to meet with us, ask questions to learn how they are doing, and find ways to serve them. When we shift from focusing on our loneliness to how we can love someone else, we'll find that the circle has been broken.

Questions to Consider:

I only listed a few challenges to community in this chapter. Did any of them resonate with you? Why? How have these challenges kept you from engaging in community?

Read Psalm 55. What was David's hope in the midst of his rejection?

Do you ever use social media as a replacement for community? Do you see why this is problematic?

ALL
CONFLICT
IN THE
CHURCH
BREAKS
OUR UNITY
WITH ONE
ANOTHER.

12

Barriers to Community

'Be kind to one another, tenderhearted, forgiving one another, as God in Christ forgave you.'
EPHESIANS 4:32

THE book of Philippians is often called the book of joy. Though Paul wrote the book while he was in prison and the Philippian church he wrote it to faced opposition, he wrote to remind them of the joy that was theirs in the gospel. No matter their circumstances, they could rejoice and stand firm because of the power of the gospel and their citizenship in heaven. After laying this groundwork, Paul transitioned to practical matters of the church. He began by mentioning two women by name:

> I entreat Euodia and I entreat Syntyche to agree in the Lord. Yes, I ask you also, true companion, help these

173

> women, who have labored side by side with me in the
> gospel together with Clement and the rest of my fellow
> workers, whose names are in the book of life (Phil. 4:2-3).

These two women served with Paul in ministry and were involved in some kind of conflict with one another. Paul urged them to do what he wrote in 2:2, 'complete my joy by being of the same mind, having the same love, being in full accord and of one mind.' He wanted them to remember their unity in Christ and with each other. He also asked some unnamed 'true companion' to help these women resolve their conflict.

This passage in Philippians is not the only one in Scripture that mentions conflict in the church. In Galatians 2, Paul mentions a conflict he had with Peter, 'But when Cephas (Peter) came to Antioch, I opposed him to his face, because he stood condemned. For before certain men came from James, he was eating with the Gentiles; but when they came he drew back and separated himself, fearing the circumcision party. And the rest of the Jews acted hypocritically along with him, so that even Barnabas was led astray by their hypocrisy' (vv. 11-13). There was also some disagreement between Paul and Mark in Acts 15. Paul did not want Mark to join them on a missionary journey because he had abandoned them on a previous journey. So Paul and Silas went one way and Mark and Barnabas another. In 1 Corinthians 3, Paul references a division in the Corinthian church where some were saying they followed Paul and others Apollos, 'For while there is jealousy and strife among you, are you not of the flesh and behaving only in a human way? For when one says, "I follow Paul," and another, "I follow Apollos," are you not being merely human?' (vv. 3-4).

As I've described various characteristics of Christian friendship, of sisterhood in the Lord, you've probably thought of all the times you've seen problems and conflicts among believers. Perhaps your mind recalled memories of church divisions, of women who have not spoken to each other in years, and of people who have left the church due to wounds inflicted by other believers. If you've been in the church any length of time, you've probably seen fellow church members, whom you love, hurt one another. You've seen people draw lines in the sand and take sides.

I have and multiple times over. My first memories of church are of a church split. I remember asking my mother to explain why our pastor and many of our friends had left our church and why we didn't see them anymore. In that case it was because of a theological difference. Since then I've been in churches where I witnessed one conflict after another, many of which resulted in large groups of people leaving the church. I've witnessed poor communication that resulted in hurt feelings. I've witnessed the impact of gossip and slander. I've seen people refuse to forgive and seek reconciliation. The difficult part of it all was seeing people I dearly loved, whom I considered family, break away from community.

Breaking Unity

As we learned at the beginning of this book, our friendship with one another is grounded in our unity with Christ and with one another. All conflict in the church breaks our unity with one another, and all such conflict is caused by sin. From the moment our first parents disobeyed God and ate from the tree, their relationship with one another was marked by conflict, as has every relationship since then.

Though we are redeemed through the blood of Christ, we still battle the presence of sin in our lives. Though we are no longer slaves to sin, we still sin. We still seek our own good above others. We still envy and covet. We are still unkind, impatient, prideful, and selfish. We fail to love God with all our heart and our neighbor as we love ourselves. When you put a group of sinners together in a church community, we sin against one another.

In the southern United States, there is an invasive vine known as Kudzu. When it takes over a group of trees, it grows and spreads so that the trees are no longer visible; all you see is the vine. When weeds of sin make their way into our fellowship, they spread, choking our unity. These sins create barriers that act like walls, blocking our love for one another. When the world looks at us, they no longer see us reflecting the love of Christ, but see our conflict instead.

Though there are many sins that can threaten our love for one another, I want to highlight a few sins we as women often struggle with. Some of these sins might be ones we perpetrate and others might be sins our sisters perpetrate against us. These sins can act like fast growing weeds that choke the life out of Christian friendship and threaten the unity of the church.

Gossip

'The words of a whisperer are like delicious morsels; they go down into the inner parts of the body' (Prov. 18:8). We all love to hear gossip; our ears prick up in anticipation at the prospect of juicy news about someone else. We devour it like our favorite candy. As soon as we can, we pass it on to the next person.

Gossip is sharing information about someone else that hurts their character in the eyes of another person. Sometimes it is true and sometimes it isn't. Regardless, it isn't our information to share. It is a sin that brings down a church. Sharing such information seems powerless; impotent. How can sharing words about someone else be so deadly? It is a poison that spreads like the common cold. We hear things about other people and shake our heads in judgment. We share our negative opinions with others and before we know it, we've influenced their thoughts of a person who isn't there to defend themselves. The person who is talked about is left defenseless and hurt.

Gossip also breaks trust between friends when a friend confides in us and we go on to share the information with others. 'Whoever goes about slandering reveals secrets, but he who is trustworthy in spirit keeps a thing covered' (Prov. 11:13). I've seen gossip cause people to leave a church because they no longer felt safe there.

Lest we think that gossip is a less serious sin compared to other sins – since it is a sin that everyone does and somehow is considered 'acceptable' among Christians – we need to remember that it is included in the list of sins in Romans 1: 'And since they did not see fit to acknowledge God, God gave them up to a debased mind to do what ought not to be done. They were filled with all manner of unrighteousness, evil, covetousness, malice. They are full of envy, murder, strife, deceit, maliciousness. They are gossips, slanderers, haters of God, insolent, haughty, boastful, inventors of evil, disobedient to parents, foolish, faithless, heartless, ruthless' (vv. 28-31). Paul also wrote in Titus that believers were, 'to speak evil of no one, to avoid quarreling, to be gentle, and to show perfect courtesy toward all people' (3:2).

Gossip separates sisters in Christ. It breaks our unity. We must avoid it at all costs. When someone starts to tell us something they've heard about someone else, even wrapped in the form of a prayer request, we need to stop it. We need to tell them to stop talking and tell them we will not participate in spreading gossip. If necessary, we need to stay away from people who are prone to gossip. When a friend confides in us, we need to keep that information to ourselves. It is not our story to give away. And if gossip is a sin we have actively participated in, we need to confess and repent of it. Instead of gossip, we need to speak only what is good and right. 'Let no corrupting talk come out of your mouths, but only such as is good for building up, as fits the occasion, that it may give grace to those who hear' (Eph. 4:29).

For those who have been wounded by gossip, know that your Savior sees and knows your sorrow. People whispered things about Him. They looked down on Him for eating with outcasts and sinners. Some told outright lies at His trial. Give Jesus your sorrows. Know that He understands. Not only that, but know that He only speaks the truth about you. He stands before the Father, interceding on your behalf, speaking of your adoption and righteousness through His blood shed for you. No matter what anyone has said about you, Jesus only says, 'You are mine. Never will I leave you, never will I forsake you.'

Idolatry in Friendship

Friendship is a good thing and a blessing. As we've learned, God created us to need one another. But like all good things and all the blessings God has given us, we can turn friendship into an idol that we worship. An idol is anything we love, worship, and place in importance above God. It is anything we look to for meaning and significance. It consumes our thoughts and energies – thoughts and energies that should be focused on God. An idol is something we look to believing it will give us something that only God can give us. Though the idols in the Bible were often constructed of stone or wood, the idols we bow down to can be anything, including money, possessions, status, people, and power. An idol can be anything we think we need to make our lives better, happier, and give our life meaning. This includes friendship.

Idolatry in all its forms is a violation of the first and second commandment: 'You shall have no other gods before me. You shall not make for yourself a carved image, or any likeness of anything that is in heaven above, or that is in the earth beneath, or that is in the water under the earth. You shall not bow down to them or serve them, for I the LORD your God am a jealous God' (Exod. 20:4-5). We make friendship an idol when we put our friendships above our relationship with God. We do that when we expect things from our friends they aren't meant to give us or be for us. When we expect our friendship to provide us the love, affirmation, acceptance, meaning, purpose, and security that should only come from our relationship with God, we are making our friendships into idols.

How do we know if a friendship has become an idol? Our responses to failed expectations speak volumes. If a friend spends time with another friend and we feel jealousy or anger, our friendship is most likely an idol. When we expect our friends to prioritize their life around us, our friendship is an idol. When we need to hear affirmation from our friends, our friendships have taken first place in our heart. When we fear losing our friendships, our friendships have become idolatrous.

Idolatry in friendship interferes with our unity in our local church. It overemphasizes one or several friendships above all the others in the Body. It pushes others away. Idolatry is also self-centered. It focuses on what our friends can do for us rather than how we can serve them. Idolatry wants all the attention and cares little for what the rest of the Body needs.

Friendships are a good thing, but they can't become our everything. God must have first place in our heart and in our affections. He must be the one to whom we turn to meet the needs of our heart. Therefore, we need to have proper boundaries with our friendships. This is a healthy thing to do. Our friends are not our Saviors. They are fallen, sinful people just like us. They are not here to fulfill all of our needs. We need to set limits with our time, our space, our energies, and our thoughts, so that our friendships do not become all consuming.

Divisions/Conflicts

In the beginning of this chapter, I shared the passage from Philippians where Paul mentions a conflict between two women. Conflict and division in the church causes great heartache and disunity. We disagree over big things and little things. We divide over theology, the color of the new carpet in the sanctuary, hiring decisions, bulletin layouts, what study is chosen for the women's Bible study, and who gets to sing the solo in the Christmas program. We hurt one another with our words, our actions, our gossip, and our indifference. We jump to conclusions, assume the worst, and give little grace.

The heart is at the heart of church conflict. The desires of our heart motivate and feed our disputes with each other (see James 4:1-4). 'Scripture places the cause of quarrels and fights at the doorstep of our heart's unmet desires, which are rooted in our selfish passions. We want what we want, and if we don't get what we want, we do things that cause further conflict. Caught up in our desires, we become blind in the depth of our selfish passions…When we fight, quarrel, hate, and devour one another in the church, our loyalty is to our desires and passions, not to God.' [1] Looking for the heart matters behind our divisions and disagreements is essential and we often need help to do that. Seeking help from those who are wise in the faith is a must because they can help us see what we can't see. As we explore those heart issues, we can know that God is at work redeeming and transforming our hearts even in the midst of our conflicts. He uses our disputes with others to sanctify us and make us more like Christ. When we face a disagreement with a sister or sisters in the Lord, we can

---

1. Barthel, Tara Klena and Edling, David V. *Redeeming Church Conflicts: Turning Crisis into Compassion and Care* (Grand Rapids: Baker Books, 2012), p. 65.

trust that such conflict can be and will be redeemed for God's glory and the good of those involved.

As we seek to work through these clashes with others, we need to turn to God's word for it provides important tools for addressing and working through them. It shows us how God desires that we resolve conflict, and His methods are often different from those of the world. The most notable passage on dealing with disputes with believers is in Matthew 18, 'If your brother sins against you, go and tell him his fault, between you and him alone. If he listens to you, you have gained your brother. But if he does not listen, take one or two others along with you, that every charge may be established by the evidence of two or three witnesses. If he refuses to listen to them, tell it to the church. And if he refuses to listen even to the church, let him be to you as a Gentile and a tax collector' (vv. 15-17). Paul reminds us in 1 Corinthians 6:1-8 that we should seek to resolve our disagreements within the church rather than outside it. Church conflict is a family matter and we need the help of our church leaders and church government to work alongside us in redeeming and restoring our conflicts.

When we speak to those with whom we have a dispute, we remember what Christ has done for us – while we were still sinners, Christ died for us. 'Put on then, as God's chosen ones, holy and beloved, compassionate hearts, kindness, humility, meekness, and patience, bearing with one another and, if one has a complaint against another, forgiving each other; as the Lord has forgiven you, so you also must forgive. And above all these put on love, which binds everything together in perfect harmony' (Col. 3:12-14).

In any conflict or division, our unity is at stake. 'From an eternal perspective, we already are reconciled with and united to our brothers and sisters in Christ. Therefore, during any church conflict, we simply strive to become who and what we already are: one in Christ. We may differ over issues and hold conflicting positions on important questions, but those temporary things pale in comparison to our unity in Christ.'[2]

Relationships with one another within the church are often messy and broken. We are all fallen people, seeking after our own desires. More often than not, we will hurt and offend each other. Yet God calls us to love one another and one of the ways we do that is by seeking to resolve and redeem our conflicts with each other.[3] As we do so, we show the world that we do indeed belong to Christ. 'Love – and the unity it attests to – is the mark Christ gave Christians to wear before the world. Only with this mark may the world know that Christians are indeed Christians and that Jesus was sent by the Father.'[4]

Opportunities for Redemption

All of these problem areas in friendship: gossip, idolatry, rejection, and division are opportunities. They are God-ordained circumstances provided for us to learn from, grow through, and be transformed by. In fact, 'God keeps

---

2. Barthel and Edling, p. 214.

3. I highly recommend *Redeeming Church Conflicts* to all believers. It is an essential tool for addressing church conflict, written by those who have labored to mediate numerous conflicts in churches.

4. Schaeffer, p. 59.

us in messy relationships for his redemptive purposes.'[5] Instead of just making our relationships better when we ask and ending our conflicts as soon as they develop, God works in the messiness of our relationship struggles to reveal our own hearts. As Tripp and Lane note, 'we would prefer that God would just change the relationship, but he won't be content until the relationship changes us too.'[6]

Many of us use relational conflicts and struggles as reasons to turn away from friendship and community. We might feel compelled to live in isolation and keep our distance from meaningful friendship. We might grow cynical about community. We might give up on community altogether. Instead, we need to engage these struggles and seek to learn what God wants to do in us through them.

Our struggles in friendship will often reveal our own sin, even in circumstances when someone has sinned against us. That's because we often respond in sinful ways to injustice and wrongs done to us. We harbor bitterness and anger against others. We gossip or slander about those who have hurt us. We withhold forgiveness. As we face the conflicts we have with our sister-friends, we need to prayerfully consider our own sin and turn to the gospel of grace for forgiveness.

These problems in friendship also provide opportunities to display the love of Christ to our sisters. As we remember our own need for God's grace, we can be gracious to our sisters. As we realize the depths of our own sin, we can be forbearing toward our sisters. As we dwell on how much

---

5. Lane and Tripp, p. 11.

6. Lane and Tripp, p. 11.

we need Christ in order to love others as He has loved us, we turn to our sisters in humility and a desire for healing and restoration.

Questions to Consider:

What kind of struggles or conflicts have you experienced in Christian friendship? How did you resolve them?

Are you currently involved in a conflict? What might God be doing in your heart?

Read 1 Corinthians 3. What does Paul say their divisions signify? (v. 3).

WHEN YOU
FEEL UNLOVED,
DISCONNECTED,
LONELY, AND
FRIENDLESS,
REMEMBER
JESUS. HE HAS
LOVED YOU
FROM BEFORE
TIME BEGAN.

13

The Perfect Friend

'O! to be able to say "Christ is my friend," is one of the sweetest things in the world.'

CHARLES SPURGEON [1]

AS we come to the end of this book, what are your thoughts on friendship with other women in the church?

This book may have brought up mixed emotions for you. It does for me. You may desire the kind of friendship and community I've described but have faced challenges in cultivating it. You may have festering wounds that continue to ache from a friend's indifference or rejection. Trusting others in your church may be hard because of past hurts. Perhaps you've been in the middle of one too

---

1. Spurgeon, Sermon 120.

many church conflicts and you are weary, cynical, and defeated.

Whatever your experience, and whatever you might experience in friendship going forward, I want to remind you of your first and perfect friend, Jesus. I started the book with Jesus and I think it is fitting to end it with Him.

In the book of Hebrews, the author compares Jesus to the prophets, priests, and kings of the past, asserting that Jesus is better. 'For Jesus has been counted worthy of more glory than Moses – as much more glory as the builder of a house has more honor than the house itself' (Heb. 3:3). In a similar vein, I want to show you why Jesus is the perfect, better, and ultimate friend.

The Perfect and Forever Friend

As you pursue friendships with your sisters in the Lord, remember Jesus, your first, true, and forever friend.

When you feel unloved, disconnected, lonely, and friendless, remember Jesus. He has loved you from before time began. 'He chose us in him before the foundation of the world, that we should be holy and blameless before him. In love he predestined us for adoption to himself as sons through Jesus Christ' (Eph. 1:4-5).

Charles Spurgeon reminds us, 'And how long has Christ loved you? That you can not tell. When the ages were not born he loved you; when this world was an infant, wrapped in the swaddling clothes of mist, he loved you; when the old pyramids had not begun to be builded, his heart was set upon you; and ever since you have been born he has had a strong affection for you. He looked on you in your cradle, and he loved you then; he was affianced to you when you were an infant of a span long, and he has loved you ever since.'[2]

When you are judged, criticized, slandered, gossiped about, and humiliated, remember that Jesus is the perfect friend who never fails you.

> For the LORD will not forsake his people; he will not abandon his heritage (Ps. 94:4).

> For I am sure that neither death nor life, nor angels nor rulers, nor things present nor things to come, nor powers, nor height nor depth, nor anything else in all creation, will be able to separate us from the love of God in Christ Jesus our Lord (Rom. 8:38-39).

> The steadfast love of the LORD never ceases; his mercies never come to an end (Lam. 3:32).

When you struggle with sin and temptation and no friends are there to encourage and help you, remember Jesus, the One who never fails to intercede for you before the Father. He gave you the gift of His Spirit to comfort, guide, and direct you. No matter what you have done or will do, His well of grace never runs dry.

> Consequently, he is able to save to the uttermost those who draw near to God through him, since he always lives to make intercession for them (Heb. 7:25).

> Who is to condemn? Christ Jesus is the one who died – more than that, who was raised – who is at the right hand of God, who indeed is interceding for us (Rom. 8:34).

---

2. Spurgeon, Sermon 120.

My little children, I am writing these things to you so that you may not sin. But if anyone does sin, we have an advocate with the Father, Jesus Christ the righteous (1 John 2:1).

If the Spirit of him who raised Jesus from the dead dwells in you, he who raised Christ Jesus from the dead will also give life to your mortal bodies through his Spirit who dwells in you (Rom. 8:11).

When your church is filled with conflict, strife, discord, and division and your heart grieves to see friendships ripped apart, remember Jesus. He died to redeem and restore all that is broken. Even now, in the midst of the conflicts around you, He is at work. He will use it for good and His glory.

And he who was seated on the throne said, 'Behold, I am making all things new.' Also he said, 'Write this down, for these words are trustworthy and true.' (Rev. 21:5).

...as Christ loved the church and gave himself up for her, that he might sanctify her, having cleansed her by the washing of water with the word, so that he might present the church to himself in splendor, without spot or wrinkle or any such thing, that she might be holy and without blemish (Eph. 5:26-27).

Jesus is your first and forever friend. He teaches you how to be friends with your sisters. He shows you what it looks like to love and serve because He first loved and served you. He reveals what it looks like to have patience and forbearance because He gives you grace upon grace. He demonstrates how to live at peace and unity with your sisters because He himself is our peace. We love our sister-friends only in so far as we know the love Christ has for us.

When friendship is hard, when church is a lonely place, when relationships let us down, we must remember our unity in Christ. Because we are united to our Savior, we can love our sisters in Christ. Even when they fail us. Even when we disagree. Even when it seems like no one cares. Our unity with Christ creates, shapes, and sustains our love for others. 'We love because he first loved us' (1 John 4:19).

Questions to Consider:

As you've come to the end of the book, what do you think of the portrait of friendship I have painted for you? How has your view of friendship with other women in the church changed?

Do you see your need for community in the local Body? What specific steps are you taking to cultivate deeper relationships in the church?

How does Christ's love for you encourage you as you go forward in pursuing and living in community with your church?

Christian Focus Publications

Our mission statement –

STAYING FAITHFUL

In dependence upon God we seek to impact the world through literature faithful to His infallible Word, the Bible. Our aim is to ensure that the Lord Jesus Christ is presented as the only hope to obtain forgiveness of sin, live a useful life and look forward to heaven with Him.

Our books are published in four imprints:

CHRISTIAN
FOCUS

Popular works including biographies, commentaries, basic doctrine and Christian living.

CHRISTIAN
HERITAGE

Books representing some of the best material from the rich heritage of the church.

MENTOR

Books written at a level suitable for Bible College and seminary students, pastors, and other serious readers. The imprint includes commentaries, doctrinal studies, examination of current issues and church history.

CF4•K

Children's books for quality Bible teaching and for all age groups: Sunday school curriculum, puzzle and activity books; personal and family devotional titles, biographies and inspirational stories – because you are never too young to know Jesus!

Christian Focus Publications Ltd,
Geanies House, Fearn, Ross-shire,
IV20 1TW, Scotland, United Kingdom.
www.christianfocus.com
blog.christianfocus.com